MW00446916

Ghosts and
Legends
of Oklahoma

Mike Ricksecker

Schiffer Publishing Ltd

4880 Lower Valley Road, Atglen, Pennsylvania 19310

Dedication

To Cathy, Chris, Logan, Dustin, and Johnny.
Also to Arielle and Robin (you're not a jinx after all).

Cover photo: Cowboy by the fire © Laura Gangi Pond. Inside photos: Scrapyard © Tomas Hajek; Masonic Emblem Lapel Pin © Warren Price; Powerful tornado © James Thew; Vintage Steam Engine © Bob Orsillo. *All photos courtesy of www.bigstockphoto.com.*

Schiffer Books are available at special discounts for bulk purchases for sales promotions or premiums. Special editions, including personalized covers, corporate imprints, and excerpts can be created in large quantities for special needs. For more information contact the publisher:

Published by Schiffer Publishing Ltd.
4880 Lower Valley Road
Atglen, PA 19310
Phone: (610) 593-1777; Fax: (610) 593-2002
E-mail: Info@schifferbooks.com

For the largest selection of fine reference books on this and related subjects,
please visit our website at: **www.schifferbooks.com**
We are always looking for people to write books on new and related subjects.
If you have an idea for a book, please contact us at **proposals@schifferbooks.com**.

This book may be purchased from the publisher.
Include $5.00 for shipping.
Please try your bookstore first.
You may write for a free catalog.

In Europe, Schiffer books are distributed by
Bushwood Books
6 Marksbury Ave.
Kew Gardens
Surrey TW9 4JF England
Phone: 44 (0) 20 8392 8585; Fax: 44 (0) 20 8392 9876
E-mail: info@bushwoodbooks.co.uk
Website: www.bushwoodbooks.co.uk

Other Schiffer Books by the Author:
Ghosts of Maryland, 978-0-7643-3423-8, $14.99

Other Schiffer Books on Related Subjects:
Lone Star Spooks: Searching for Ghosts in Texas, 978-0-7643-3744-4, $16.99
Haunted Austin, Texas, 978-0-7643-3298-2, $14.99
Supernatural Texas: A Field Guide, 978-0-7643-3309-5, $24.99
America's Historic Haunts, 978-0-7643-3700-0, $29.99

Copyright © 2011 by Mike Ricksecker
Unless otherwise noted, all images are the property of the author.
Library of Congress Control Number: 2011932008

Designed by Mark David Bowyer
Type set in Bison / New Baskerville BT

ISBN: 978-0-7643-3943-1
Printed in the United States of America

Contents

Acknowledgments

The author appreciates the invaluable help and/or inspiration of the following people and organizations:

The Oklahoma Historical Society; *The Oklahoman*; Oklahoma State University Library; Elk City Carnegie Library; Oklahoma Office of Geographic Information; University of Tulsa; Society of the Haunted including Cathy Nance, Chris Borthick, Logan Corelli, Taylor Nance, Dustin Cupit, Johnny Longan, Andrew Shanor, and Vanessa Hogle; Christy Clark; Al Ritter of the 101 Ranch Old Timers' Association; Becky Luker of the Stone Lion Inn; Lindsey Ladd; Travis Flippin; Kent Otey; Becky Wall; Collin, Arielle, Chase, and Cameron Ricksecker; Dinah Roseberry; Gail Ricksecker (for my first ghost book, *Yankee Ghosts*, by Hans Holzer); and my wife, Robin Genelle, without whose continued love, support, and putting up with those extra late nights none of this would be possible.

Introduction

In August 2009, I moved my family out of Maryland and into the state of Oklahoma. It was a big change for us considering we had lived in Maryland since the very end of 1995, first at Ft. George G. Meade when I was still a member of the U.S. Air Force and just a few years later in Frederick. The reason was two-fold. We were getting closer to my wife's family in Oklahoma, and the economy in Maryland had taken its toll on our budget to the point that we could no longer bear it.

From a writing standpoint it was awkward since I had just submitted my completed manuscript of *Ghosts of Maryland* to Schiffer Publishing, which meant I was going to have to market a published work about the state of Maryland from Oklahoma. While this aspect may have been a bit troublesome, there was wonderful development that came from this move and it is now in your hand.

Writing *Ghosts and Legends of Oklahoma* was a fantastic way to learn about my new state of residence. Hours upon hours of research and talking to people all across Oklahoma allowed me to really appreciate the history of the state and the colorful past, both wonderful and tragic, it has had. This book serves as a cross-section of Oklahoma history from a paranormal point of view. From Native Americans, to the Civil War, to gun-slinging outlaws, to land rushes, to railroads, to cowboys, cowgirls, and Wild West shows, to tornadoes, to historic Route 66 — there's a bit of everything in this book.

I also became a part of Oklahoma Paranormal Research and Investigations (OKPRI) while I was in the middle of writing this manuscript, and became close to a number of its ghost hunting veterans. Their expertise in the paranormal field and the history of haunted locations across the state was an immense help in completing this work. Most of us have now become the Society of the Haunted, and personal accounts of their experiences will be featured "Ghost Hunting in Oklahoma" chapter. What you will not find here is a score of ghost stories about the haunted residences we have investigated as a group since there is a confidentiality pact with the homeowners we help. With OKPRI, and now the Society of the Haunted, I have also been receiving a more up-close and personal view of the paranormal that I simply didn't have with *Ghosts of Maryland*, so I think what you'll read here will be a much better account both historically and paranormally.

With this combination of historic and paranormal research, I have come to think that what I've become is a "ghostorian," which is, I believe, someone who investigates the history and origins of a ghost and the location that it haunts. That is pretty good summation of what I do, and it is what you will find within these pages.

I've put this book together a little differently than my previous work. I first have a section devoted to each Guthrie and Oklahoma City. Guthrie is just filled to the brim with haunts and really deserves its own book. The entire historic downtown is loaded with paranormal activity around every street corner. Oklahoma City has great history as well, but its populous is really what gives it such a number of stories. For neither city could I include them all here.

The next four sections break the state out into geographical regions: northeast, southeast, northwest, and southwest. This was intended to keep the reader's attention to one general area of the state and it helps in utilizing the maps in the atlas. Following those sections, I've included chapters on cemeteries, ghost towns, and ghost hunting. The cemeteries and ghost towns section round out the type of history and paranormal activity that is experienced in Oklahoma. The ghost hunting section, meanwhile, is different than the ghost hunting section I wrote in my last book, which covered the field in general terms. With the basics already addressed there, this time I focused on paranormal investigation specifically in the state of Oklahoma.

The biggest surprise for me while I conducted my research was the sheer number of ghost stories throughout the state. With Oklahoma only having been settled about a quarter of the amount of time as Maryland, I thought I was going to really have my work cut out for me in tracking down material. That was not the case. There have been a plethora of ghost stories and legends with which to work, and even as I put the finishing touches on this manuscript I still came across fantastic tales.

I think it's the nature of the beast that as you continue to dig and explore, hidden treasures become unearthed. It is my hope that you enjoy these gems I uncovered in Oklahoma during my first year of living in the state.

Part 1
Guthrie

Chapter One

Outlaw Ghosts of the Black Jail and Boot Hill

There are enough ghost stories originating from Guthrie, Oklahoma, and the surrounding area that one could easily write an entire book on just its haunts alone. Guthrie was once just a stop along the Santa Fe Railway, but when the land run hit in April 1889, it became a city of 10,000 virtually overnight. The original state capital of Oklahoma, Guthrie lost its seat in 1910, although it is now known as the Bed and Breakfast Capital of Oklahoma.

In the late nineteenth century, prior to Oklahoma becoming a state, the territory was rampant with outlaws, gunslingers, and notorious gangs of the day. To help thwart the lawlessness and disorder, one of the first Federal prisons in the Midwest was built in Guthrie in 1892, and it has lived a storied existence ever since.

Due to the impoverished conditions, early inmates dubbed the prison "The Black Jail," and the nickname has stood the test of time. The prison only had the capacity to hold ninety prisoners, but it held some notorious ones, including the Dalton Gang (although some descendants of the Dalton family contend the gang was never at The Black Jail) and Bill Doolin. The structure featured eighteen-inch thick walls, solitary confinement, and a gallows was constructed across the street when necessary. There were periodic prison breaks, and locals from times past questioned the validity of the claim that escapees Doolin, the notorious "Dynamite Bill," and Syd Wyatt were gunned down for resisting arrest. Perhaps their temporary freedom was a territorial death sentence.

The Black Jail's existence as a prison didn't last long. As Oklahoma became more settled and organized, the need for a federal penitentiary waned, and in 1908 the United States transferred the jail to the control of Logan County. Shortly thereafter, its days as a prison ended and a local chapter of the Nazarene Church took control of the property. They remodeled much of the face of the building and operated out of the church until the 1970s. The building then sat unoccupied for a number of years until it was taken over by the notorious Samaritan Foundation cult.

The existence of the Samaritan Foundation in Guthrie was unknown until a man from Massachusetts came to town in 1993 seeking his two children. Their mother had run off with the two to Oklahoma, claiming it was going to be a ten-day "chance of a lifetime," but over the course of the next month she never returned and the man was only able to talk to his children for a total of twelve minutes over the phone. He stated his wife had been acting in a bizarre fashion for eighteen months, ever since she'd starting receiving literature from the cult. Stating she was trying to remove

The Black Jail silently awaits further restoration.

evil, the woman would swing a pendulum over the children, place a circular drawing over Universal Price Codes, and would place the same drawing under the children's pillows at night. Literature from the organization urged members not to talk on the phone because vampires could gain access to them, and it claimed President Clinton was "an animal mutant zombie." The operation was shut down in 1995. The old prison has remained vacant ever since, but work to restore the facility is slowly underway.

The most popular ghostly tale of The Black Jail is that of James Phillips. In June 1907, Phillips was sentenced to the noose, the first white man to be hanged in fifteen years of the prison's existence. On the eve of his date with death, he stared out of his window as he painfully watched the carpenters assemble the gallows. According to the prison guards on duty, Phillips suddenly fell back from the window and onto his bunk without a word and died that very moment. The coroner was baffled and simply placed in his report that the prisoner had died of fright. Apparently, Phillips just scared the soul out of his own body, because the outlaw can still be spotted walking the corridors of the prison's basement. Preservationists have seen dark shadows near the cell where it is said Phillips died, and passersby on the street have claimed to spot a man peering out of one of the lower level windows.

The traditional story of James Phillips maintains that the gallows built for him were constructed on the other side of Noble Avenue, across from the jail. Some locals believe that they were actually constructed across 2nd Street, where a house now stands. This house is also said to have been used by the Samaritan Foundation as well as a staging point for the 1995 Oklahoma City bombing, and odd occurrences have kept the home restless, although the tenants at the time wished not to delve into the details.

Another popular sighting around The Black Jail is the apparition of a young woman that likes to cross Noble Avenue around the time of dusk.

Some say she was once a prostitute who came to service the prisoners, but others contend that she appears too sophisticated for such a line of work and must be a patron of the old Nazarene Church. Whichever the case may be, she has periodically disrupted traffic on the street as a number of drivers have slowed down or stopped to let the woman pass only to watch her vanish. Witnesses say she wears a long printed dress, a large brimmed hat, and gloves. Some also credit this apparition with a woman's voice that can be heard singing along the main floor of the building, but it's possible that this could be an entirely different spirit.

Many of the area's outlaws and prisoners of the Black Jail were buried in the Boot Hill section of Summit View Cemetery on the north side of Guthrie. Bill Doolin is buried there, as well as fellow outlaws Charlie Pierce, Richard "Little Dick" West, and Bert Casey. Buried next to Doolin is the legendary outlaw Elmer McCurdy.

One of Boot Hill's famous burial plots, McCurdy is more legendary for his post-life adventures rather than his criminal career. In fact, he had planned to rob a train carrying a considerable amount of money but instead botched the job and robbed the one before it, which netted only had $46. He and his gang also made off with the train's whiskey. McCurdy was an outlaw of moderate notoriety and died drunk in a shoot-out with deputy sheriffs at a barn near the Oklahoma-Kansas border in 1911, and he likely would have been utterly forgotten except that no one came to claim his body.

Unsure what to do with Elmer McCurdy, the local mortician in Pawhuska, Oklahoma, propped up his corpse in a corner and awaited claim. According to Arthur H. Lamb's *Tragedies of the Osage Hills* (no official publication date, but the work dates to the early 1900s), "His body was dressed in the rough clothes he wore when killed and stood up in the corner of the local morgue where it remained for five years. Thousands viewed it but no one identified it."

Finally, two men from California that claimed to be McCurdy's brothers made off with the body and covered it in wax to become part of a traveling sideshow. Years later it was painted to glow in the dark, and the body hung from a noose in an amusement park fun house in Long Beach, California. McCurdy's corpse shrunk and mummified; nobody remembered that he was real, simply calling him "The Dummy."

More than sixty-five years after his death, he was discovered in 1976 during the filming of an episode of *The Six Million Dollar Man* when a worker moved McCurdy and the mummy's arm fell off. Seeing the skeleton inside, he notified authorities and created a stir that made headlines. While a Los Angeles County coroner examined the body, research began to determine whom it belonged to. Once convinced this was the body of Elmer McCurdy, it was transported to Guthrie to be buried with other outlaws of his time and ilk.

Chapter Two

Blue Belle and the Bordello

The historic bar bustles with activity in the pale moonlight. A brown-haired man with a handlebar mustache and brown derby hat saunters across the room and nods at an attractive brunette on his way to the stairs leading down to the basement. She nods back as he turns from her, but he scoffs a random obscenity as he disappears into the darkness below. She has no idea what got stuck in his craw, although his craw usually gets stuck for no apparent reason. He's been like that for a long time, this guy. Perhaps the quiet gentleman in the corner who just comes in to people-watch finally annoyed him, but it really doesn't concern her as long as ol' Handlebars keeps paying. It also doesn't concern her that the two girls upstairs are whimpering again. They're like that sometimes, bawling like babies, sometimes even blubbering for help, but one of these days they'd grow out of it. She had a business to run, after all, and if they didn't shape up she just might have to knock some sense in to them — or someone else just might do that for her if they keep it up at this rate. For now, she sits and touches up her raven dark hair as she awaits a visit from a family who is having financial problems and needs her help. However, the doors are locked and not a living soul is actually inside the Blue Belle Saloon.

What unseen patrons from long ago still pull up to the Blue Belle's bar for a phantom drink? *Courtesy of Cathy Nance*.

The original establishment on the corner of Harrison Avenue and 2nd Street was a collection of tents set up by John Sampsel. He moved to Oklahoma from Kansas with his family during the land run and staked his claim. Soon, he was having supplies brought in by wagon and he set up a restaurant and cigar stand under the tents in 1889, which he called the Blue Belle. During the early 1890s, a wood frame building was constructed to replace the tents and house the saloon. Unfortunately for Sampsel, he mismanaged his finances and lost the property in a sheriff's auction to Joseph J. Hein in May 1896.

Operating at the same location was Miss Lizzie's Girls, a group of frontier prostitutes run by their Madame, Miss Lizzie. By all accounts, Lizzie was an intelligent church-going woman who kept a fine reputation, however, she would accept very young girls into the profession. Local legends maintain that families about to lose their homes would sell their young daughters into the service of Miss Lizzie and put them to work in her bordello.

During this time, "Wild Bill" Doolin and his gang of "Wild Bunch" outlaws were known to frequent the saloon, get liquored up, and gamble. They spent the better part of four years robbing trains and banks throughout Indian Territory until their apprehension in June 1896. They were held at the Federal prison in Guthrie, also known as The Black Jail, until July 5th of the same year when Doolin orchestrated a mass breakout. Thirty-seven prisoners escaped, but Doolin and the Wild Bunch would never again raise their glasses at the Blue Belle. A posse led by Heck Thomas hunted down Doolin and found him in Lawton, where Thomas gunned down the outlaw in a firefight. Over the next few years the rest of the gang was hunted down as well.

Other notorious gangs that were rumored to have stopped by the Blue Belle include the Dalton Gang, High Fives Gang, and the Cook Gang. Opposing these outlaws were the "Three Guardsmen" — Heck Thomas, Chris Madsen, and Bill Tilghman — who likely stopped at the Blue Belle when they were in Guthrie, but they spent much of their time in Perry, which had earned the title of "Hell's Half Acre" after a land run brought tens of thousands of people into the area and over one hundred saloons sprouted up almost overnight. Taming the Wild West was a daunting task, and a refreshing drink after dropping off a few prisoners at the Guthrie Federal territorial prison was certainly understandable.

After Joseph Hein sold the Blue Belle to the Ferd Hein Brewing Company based in Kansas City, Missouri, the Fremont Land and Improvement Company bought the establishment in 1901 and replaced the original framed building with the brick and mortar one that stands there today. The substantially increased size of the building was spacious enough for a seventeen-room second floor, which housed a gambling den and a full-fledged bordello for Miss Lizzie. This was more of a private club and was not generally open to the public, but both outlaws and local authority figures are said to have ventured up the east side stairwell to the second floor. There was also a private iron catwalk from the upstairs bordello that stretched over the road to the hotel across the street where local politicians and affluent visitors had access to the prostitutes. Although there's no confirmation one way or the other if they ever ventured up to the second floor, the legends that at least walked through the front door of the Blue Belle include Will Rogers, William Wrigley, and President Theodore Roosevelt.

Legendary early twentieth century actor, Tom Mix, actually tended bar at the Blue Belle Saloon, beginning in 1902 after moving to Guthrie with his wife. Local ranchers who stopped in learned that Tom was also a wrangler and bronco buster, and soon he was befriending Zack Mulhall and George and Zach Miller of the famous 101 Ranch, all of whom helped launch Mix's successful career.

Major problems arose for the Blue Belle Saloon when Oklahoma entered statehood in 1907. In part to keep liquor from American Indians and partly based on strong southern conservative religious values, Oklahoma became the only state to write prohibition into their constitution, and they entered the union as a dry state. All existing saloons were formally shut down, although many former proprietors ran successful bootlegging operations. They were so successful, in fact, that Will Rogers once quipped, "Oklahoma will be a dry state as long as the voters can stagger to the polls."

For many years, the Blue Belle building was host to a variety of stores under a number of different ownerships, but nothing really stuck and the building was usually vacant. Perhaps the restless spirits there couldn't see it as anything other than their old watering hole and drove out the shopkeepers. When state prohibition was lifted in 1959, the building was again purchased, but it was finally restored to its former glory and, in 1977, officially renamed the Blue Belle Saloon. It has operated under that moniker ever since.

With a bustling historic bar comes bustling historic ghosts — and a number have been spotted over the years. The apparition of a man has frequently been seen in different areas of the saloon, including the bar and around the restroom. Many women feel uneasy in the restroom, and many refuse to use it at all. A dark haired woman has been seen many times throughout the bar area as well, and people believe this is the spirit of Miss Lizzie.

The basement has seen its share of paranormal activity with objects *physically* moving of their own accord. One time, upon entering the basement the owner saw one of the lights above a pool table swaying from side to side. It then stopped of its own accord and began swaying forward and backward. The owner then called out to whatever entity may be there to stop, and if he or she didn't stop then there would be consequences to face. The light suddenly stopped moving. In another incident, a beer glass suddenly slid across one of the tables. There is also the spirit of a disgruntled man with a handlebar mustache and a brown derby hat that is sometimes present in the basement hurling obscenities at those who enter.

Upstairs in the bordello, movement of unknown origins is often detected, and loud knocks and thumps emanate throughout. Shadows can be seen moving from room to room and disembodied voices are heard, including humming and singing occasionally. Sometimes the soft sound of a girl crying permeates the air, and this has been attributed to both Claudia and Estelle, girls that once worked for Miss Lizzie.

Estelle was sold into Miss Lizzie's services at the young age of fifteen, but what became of her no one knows for sure. Claudia was also sold to Miss Lizzie to save her family's farm from foreclosure, but she was so vocally opposed to the arrangement that her welcome as one of Miss Lizzie's girls soon soured. The Blue Belle legend is that Claudia was beaten to death and buried within the saloon by the old coal chute. Near the chute is rumored to be an entrance to the old labyrinth of tunnels under Guthrie, which would have been used by prominent patrons of the Blue Belle and bordello that did not wish to be seen. It would have been a perfect exit for a getaway by whoever may have murdered the girl. Whether or not the murder really happened no one knows for sure, but the spectral cries that emanate from that location have many convinced of her unfortunate demise.

Chapter Three

Santa Fe Depot

In the late 1800s, the territory that is now Oklahoma started to become connected to the rest of the country by railroad. Completed in 1887 with just a single track, the Santa Fe Railway became the only line into the territory and the town of Guthrie was simply a watering station with a small wood frame building that temporarily served as a depot. As the importance of Guthrie grew, so did its need for bigger rail facilities, and in 1903 a two-story red brick station was built. It handled passenger and mail service, and contained a newsstand, railroad offices, employee living quarters, and a Harvey House restaurant.

The Harvey House was a nineteenth century franchise operation of the Fred Harvey Company and is considered to be the first restaurant chain in America. Prior to dining cars becoming commonplace on passenger lines, freight agent Fred Harvey thought it would be prudent to install restaurants with high quality food at stations instead of letting passengers fend for themselves at the ramshackle roadhouses along the countryside. The first Harvey House began operation in Topeka, Kansas, in 1876, and was an instant success. Ten years later, one of these restaurants was installed every one hundred miles along the Santa Fe Railway.

Harvey also believed in quality service to go along with quality food, but when travelers treated the African American service horribly, he instituted a new policy in 1883. Only single, well-mannered, educated young women between ages eighteen and thirty would be hired as a "Harvey Girl" to serve the customers. They were paid well, but they were relegated to a strict dress code: starched black and white uniform with "Elsie" collars, opaque black stockings, and black shoes. The girls' hair had to be maintained in a net and tied with a white ribbon, and makeup was prohibited. The girls became popular enough that Harvey aprons were sold commercially, a 1942 book *The Harvey Girls* was written by Samuel Hopkins Adams, and a 1946 film based on the book and starring Judy Garland and Angela Lansbury was produced.

The Santa Fe Depot at Guthrie has had both a historic and colorful past. The most historic moment that the station witnessed was the day the capital of Oklahoma was officially transferred from Guthrie to Oklahoma City. On December 29, 1910, Governor Charles N. Haskell met with his attorney W. A. Ledbetter at the Harvey House for a cup of coffee and at 8:40 p.m. he signed the legislation. It was a devastating moment for the denizens of Guthrie, and they held animosity against Oklahoma City and its denizens for decades.

Harvey girls of yesteryear still serve guests at the old Santa Fe Depot.

Seventeen years prior, there was a different type of Guthrie catastrophe going on in the Harvey House. Patrons of the restaurant screamed and ran out of the building in terror in the summer of 1893, when small live toads were found kicking about in the hot coffee they were served. The manager, John W. Wiker, was outraged and did his best to placate the customers. Some laughed it off while others were incensed. The outbreak of toads all carefully placed in the coffee mugs was obviously a prank pulled off by one of the employees, but for sixty years it remained a mystery as to who had pulled it off. Wiker grilled the employees after the train pulled out, and Santa Fe officials launched an investigation with vice-presidents and superintendents rushing down from Chicago. However, everyone had an ironclad alibi. It was finally revealed in 1953 that the brakeman of a freight train that had also pulled in that morning, Snyder, a practical joker who longed to annoy the prominent patrons of the restaurant, had collected a number of tiny toads that were hopping about the large water tank that was supplying the engine. No one paid him any attention when he came in for coffee minutes later, and with enough sleight of hand he managed to populate the other coffee mugs with the toads. Unfortunately, the waitresses were too busy to notice the tiny intruders and the toads perished in the hot coffee they poured.

A local legend of the Santa Fe line was John Fogarty for whom the Fogarty Junior High School of Guthrie was named. From 1905 until his death in 1923, Fogarty was the conductor of the No. 410 passenger train, which was known in its day as "Four Hundred and Fogarty." During the turbulent days of Oklahoma's past with outlaw gangs, boomtowns, and gun-wielding ranch hands, the Four Hundred and Fogarty had the reputation for being the most reliable locomotive on the railway. Tales of Fogarty's toughness, including a few incidents in which pistols were drawn, made the rounds. Nobody got the best of the popular conductor.

The Santa Fe Railway was not without its tragedies in Guthrie either. In May 1936, a faulty rail just three miles north of the depot caused a horrific train wreck on the bridge over the Cimarron River. Although it's hard to use the phrase "fortunately" when there are deaths involved, it was quite fortunate that while the locomotive and twelve cars left the train tracks, only one plunged twenty-five feet into the river swollen by recent storms. Railway express agency manager L. R. Guiff of Kansas City, Missouri, and Ramon McNulty, a resident of Guthrie and Guiff's helper, both perished in the accident. One of the other cars was balanced half over the river, but none of the other passengers received serious injuries.

On May 19, 1954, a Santa Fe locomotive halted at Guthrie remained at a standstill instead of continuing its journey on the railway after what was supposed to be a twenty-minute stopover. It was soon discovered that its engineer, John Avery, had died of a heart attack while waiting. While he had become a locomotive engineer in 1921, his career with Santa Fe had begun at Guthrie in 1910, perhaps as a fitting bookend to his demise forty-four years later.

As transportation around the nation evolved, so did the Santa Fe Depot. In 1971, Amtrak took control of the railway, and the classic red-and-silver Santa Fe colors were replaced the red-and-blue of the modern line. By 1979, however, Amtrak ended its services in Oklahoma and the cessation of freight operation followed a few months later, so the depot was without a working railway. It remained this way for almost twenty years.

A restoration project was proposed in the mid-1980s, but the deal fell through. A more serious endeavor was launched in the late 1990s with a remodeling in 1997 by the local historical society. In 2002, it was purchased by Gordon Neff, who reopened the depot with a pastry shop modeled after the old Harvey House, an event center, and a model railroad museum. By the end of the decade, however, mortgage problems caused some ownership wrangling and the facility was lost to new owners who took possession of the museum and sold off many of its contents. The pastry shop was converted into a restaurant, though the event center has remained as it was. They host birthdays, weddings, and even Elvis has been spotted there.

While the first floor construction of the depot has been updated in its restoration, the basement is relatively untouched with its old coal-burning furnace still standing intact and the old coal chute remaining but boarded up. The second floor, which was used by the Harvey Girls as a dormitory, has had some remodeling completed, but is not currently used. Also hidden on the premises is the old access point to Guthrie's tunnels. Prominent business men would get off the train and use these tunnels to travel to buildings they may not have wanted the public to see them going, such as a local bordello.

Most of the paranormal activity at the Santa Fe depot centers around the second floor dormitory. A woman in a long, black Victorian dress is often seen there and it's believed that she is the woman who supervised the Harvey Girls. For quite time there were those that believed this woman to be Fred Harvey's wife; however, the Harvey's lived in Kansas City where the company was headquartered and not at the Guthrie station. It is likely that this woman served as a type of headmistress for the Harvey Girls and is commonly seen in spirit as the stern and authoritative type. Still to this day trying to keep her girls wholesome, she becomes frosty when male visitors venture up to take a peek at where the girls once lived.

Downstairs in the depot area is a bit of residual energy from passengers of long ago. This plays back like a recorder and gives the occasional snapshot of the train station from the past with voices and noises coming back to life at seemingly random moments. Are some of the strange things that are heard remnants of the toads in the coffee cups chaos? Perhaps one of the voices is that of conductor John Fogarty or engineer John Avery. There may also be an intelligent haunt on the first level as well since employees of the restaurant have found drinks filled on tables and chairs pulled out as an invitation to sit down when the setting hadn't been there moments before.

Mid-America Paranormal Science investigated the depot in 2008 and discovered an interesting anomaly in the basement, although there hadn't been very many previous reports of activity there. With their video equipment they captured a white mist forming in a room, and after formation it floated to a nearby wall and disappeared. This video footage was aired on Discover Oklahoma.

The old Santa Fe Depot in Guthrie is a quaint look back at the formation of Oklahoma when locomotives were first brought into the territory. It has served the town in both good times and bad, and it continues to serve Guthrie well as a small tourist attraction. If you stop in for lunch one day at the restaurant, you might actually be served by a Harvey Girl from one hundred years ago.

Chapter Four

Masonic Children's Home

Heart racing, she trudged up the stone walkway to the front of the massive brick mansion where her entire being felt even heavier. Sadness riddled the air, and the burden became more oppressive as she dragged her body toward the figures. A fountain loomed in front of her and to the left sat the weathered effigy of a boy and a girl sitting on a park bench. The vision of it should have been harmless, cute even, but she wanted to burst into tears.

The Temple of the Scottish Rite of Freemasonry in Guthrie is one of the largest Masonic centers in the world. Harper Samuel Cunningham, a thirty-three degree Mason, wanted to ensure the fraternal architecture was prominent in the seat of Territorial government when he made the Run of the Unassigned Lands in 1889, and that was in Guthrie at the time. Although the state capital was later moved to Oklahoma City, the Masonic Fraternity maintained its presence in Guthrie and expanded there. This included more than just the Temple.

The Masonic Children's Home looms at the end of Elm Street.

The Masonic Children's Home, now known as Dominion House, was opened in 1923, and for the first four years of its existence it housed both the children and the elderly. This combination caused quite a bit of chaos between the two disparate age groups. Grand Master Henry S. Johnston noted, "Elderly men smoke and chew and swear and old men and elderly men and elderly women both grouch and complain, and the very playfulness which makes a boy the delight of a parent, the sunbeam of a home, renders him an object of aversion to some elderly persons who are not related to the boy or interested in him, especially when his noise and play clashes with their past habits of life or the condition of nerves of the elderly person."

After it became strictly a children's home, a number of strange tales started surfacing from the there. One concerns a head mistress that was ruthless and ended up killing a number of the children. A six year-old girl is supposed to have been beaten to death by her, and it's said that the headmistress buried four boys in the basement. Another legend states that a nurse hung herself in the bell tower. A small collection of graves was reportedly discovered behind the home after the house was vacated in 1978, but the official word is that there are no graves on the property. It's difficult to say what is and isn't true about the facility, since if something ominous did happen, a society like the Masons would certainly do its best to keep it under wraps.

Today the home serves as a gorgeous event center and is a perfect location for a couple in love wishing to have an elegant wedding in a beautifully manicured garden. However, the couple may have some uninvited guests that attend.

During renovation, construction workers often heard unexplainable footsteps throughout the building and at times saw apparitions that would suddenly appear and then disappear a moment later. The most common was that of a little girl seemingly pleading for protection. Some local children claimed to have played with the various spirits of the children at the home when it was rundown and abandoned. Other strange noises would echo throughout the structure, including that of children crying, and many times the workers felt as if they were being watched by something unearthly.

The haunt that has intrigued most people is that of the belltower of the Masonic Children's Home. For decades, the legend of the nurse who hung herself there also includes her restless spirit haunting the tower. Some variations of this tale, however, state that it was a maintenance man who hanged himself. In either case, a dark shadow has been seen lurking in the belltower, and those that broke in to the home during the years it sat dormant professed that this shadow would hover near them when they ventured near. To this day, people claim that they see a dark shadow moving about up there, and visitors long to traverse up to investigate.

During a visit to Dominion House, my wife, daughter, and I ventured around to the front of the building to take a few snapshots of the stoic architecture. The entire time we were out front my wife felt sadness and a heaviness...as if she was being spiritually repressed. This became even more pronounced around the fountain area near which sat a statue of a young boy and girl sitting on a park bench. She felt as if something horrible had happened there, but she couldn't discern what it may have been. As we walked back around the side of the building, the repression lightened. Could she have been feeling the pain of the children who had been rumored to perish there? There are many mysteries still to uncover at the old Masonic Children's Home.

Chapter Five

Logan County Memorial Hospital

Abandoned, empty, and decrepit, the old Logan County Memorial Hospital stands at on the west side of Guthrie as a monument to desolation. Its windows are either cracked or boarded up and its façade is crumbling, but hope still remains that it may be restored, ghosts and all.

Construction on the building began in 1925, but it was soon halted due to the financial constraints of the Methodist Episcopal Conference, which funded the project. The hospital was going to be a state-of-the-art medical facility, but that dream was never realized. In 1946, the Order of the Sisters of Saint Benedict purchased the nearly twenty-year-old vacant eyesore, completed the hospital's construction through a grant from the Katherine E. Price Foundation, and opened it as the Benedictine Heights Hospital.

Logan County Memorial Hospital continues to decay.

Although no longer the dream cutting-edge facility, the hospital was reputable and served the area well for thirty years. The Sisters of St. Francis purchased the hospital in 1964, renaming it the Alvero Heights Hospital and then, later, Logan County Memorial Hospital. In 1972, they sold the hospital to the Logan County Hospital Authority who ran it until 1978 while a new local health facility was constructed. The doors of the five story building have remained closed to the public ever since, but the public has a hard time staying out.

Local authorities have had numerous breaking and entering problems with teens and others that are curious about the old relic. Some weeks the Guthrie police will arrest upwards of ten people for trespassing in the antiquated hospital, but what keeps drawing the trespassers there in the first place?

From the street, many in the area have seen the image of a person walking about on the third floor...possibly a former Sister still watching over the property. People that have stayed in the building at night and have ventured up to the top floor "Nun's Quarters" have felt unnerving sensations and chills up their spines for no explainable reason. A few have even claimed to have been grabbed by an unseen hand on that level or have seen a strange red light dancing about the halls. What kind of message the Sisters of the past are trying to send is unknown, but visitors do not stay up there for very long.

Most people admit to sensing a feeling of dread when they first enter the old hospital. Cries and voices can be heard emanating from the building both inside and out, disembodied and unsettling. A tunnel from the bottom level of the hospital leads to what had been a local mortuary across the street. The feeling of dread increases there, and shadow figures have been spotted lurking throughout the entire basement.

Rumors for years have percolated that Logan County Memorial is going to be restored and used as an apartment complex, but it still remains a specter on Guthrie's west end.

Chapter Six

The Stone Lion Inn

The house is rarely quiet. Something is always moving; something is always lurking. As we neared the bottom landing of the staircase in the bowels of the lurid night, having just declared we were setting forth to venture up, silence suddenly enveloped the entire structure. We took a step up and our breath caught in the back of our throats when a door on the second floor creaked open.

The Stone Lion Inn is a fantastic bed and breakfast decorated in the style and panache of the early twentieth century. It features six different suites, a library, and parlors both upstairs and down. It also features an oak paneled dining room and a gorgeous Adam-style staircase. Located on the west side of Guthrie, the mansion also hosts one of the preeminent murder mystery experiences in the state.

The historic Stone Lion Inn is one of the most haunted houses in Oklahoma.

Historically, the Stone Lion Inn was built in 1907 by the Houghton family; with six children, they were outgrowing their smaller abode on the lot next door. Fred E. Houghton made the run into Oklahoma in 1889, coming in on the second train into the territory, was the founder of the Cotton Oil Company, the owner of the first car dealership in Oklahoma, the F. E. Houghton Motor Co., and a member of Guthrie's first city council. He was a key figure in installing the town's first water works, street surveying, and building schools.

Houghton was also one of the accused in what was known as "The Cotton Gin Cases" in 1909, a series of cases in which local businessmen were indicted by a grand jury for conducting a pool in Logan County for the control and regulation of the cotton trade. However, Houghton's case was dismissed when the first case in the series against W. H. Coyle returned a "not guilty" verdict in 1913.

During their time at the Stone Lion Inn, the Houghtons had five more children. Unfortunately, one of their young daughters was over-medicated with opium-laced cough syrup (a common remedy in those days) by one of the maids. For many years, locals and paranormal investigators who encountered her spirit at the Stone Lion Inn thought this child to be Augusta Houghton. However, when The Atlantic Paranormal Society (TAPS) investigated the Stone Lion Inn for the *Ghost Hunters* television show, they discovered that Augusta had grown to adulthood and lived a long life. TAPS found a record of a young child that died at the old house in 1897, but the name was listed as "unknown" and was four years old. It's possible that this child may have followed the family in spirit to the new mansion.

There's a possibility that the child spirit could be Irene, a baby listed in the Houghton family for the 1910 census, but not listed at all for the 1920 census. There was also a photo featured in a local newspaper in 1916 that showed Mrs. Houghton and four of her children, but none of the four were Irene. In fact, the photo included the two children born prior to Irene and the two born after.

Financial instability hit the family in the 1920s when the cotton crop was struck by boll weevils. The result was that the family left their house in Guthrie and moved to Enid where they owned a mercantile. In their stead, Smith's Funeral Home leased the mansion from the Houghton's and used it as a mortuary for eight years.

The Houghton family returned in the early 1930s. In 1943, Fred E. Houghton died in the home two weeks after suffering a stroke. With her husband gone and her children grown, Bertha Houghton ran a rooming and boarding house out of the house until she finally passed away in 1958.

The house was sold into the control of the Walker family and it remained theirs until 1986, when Becky Luker came along and wanted to use the old relic as a bed and breakfast as well as a personal residence for her and her sons. A bed and breakfast hadn't existed before in Oklahoma, and the concept was foreign to the local community. That, on top of the recessed Oklahoman economy at the time, made it a tough go for the family.

It wasn't long before the antics started up. The restoration crew stayed overnight at the house during the project and heard odd noises at night. Sometimes, doors would open and close on their own in front of them. Becky shrugged it off and when the restoration was complete, she opened the bed and breakfast. She didn't even realize that the table that had been left behind in the kitchen was an old embalming table from the home's mortuary days. For that matter, she didn't even realize that house had once been a mortuary.

Mystery solved. It was Mr. Ricksecker in the library with the camera.

For a time, one of Luker's sons had a toy closet on the third floor and he started accusing his mother of rearranging the toys on him. Frustrated, he put a lock on the door to keep her out but discovered that the toys would still get rearranged. He was a straight-forward, matter-of-fact child, and when he finally said that he had seen the apparition of the little girl spirit, Becky had no doubt in her mind that he was telling the truth.

The bed and breakfast was failing as the general creepiness of the house, mixed with the unusual experiences customers were having, kept people at bay. Becky was brainstorming for ideas to make her business work and she'd heard that back east murder mystery dinner theaters were quite popular. She tried her hand at writing one, and when she unveiled it the new theme for the Stone Lion Inn was a success.

With the increased popularity of the house, reports about unusual activity began flooding from it. Footsteps emanated throughout the house and doors continued to open and slam shut on their own. Antique dolls in the bedroom where the young Houghton girl had stayed would suddenly be covered up with blankets. Word spread, and the Stone Lion Inn was featured in a *Daily Oklahoman* article just before Halloween in 1989, "Guthrie Homes Ghostly."

As the notoriety of the Stone Lion Inn continued to grow, so did the popularity of the bed and breakfast industry in Oklahoma, particularly in Guthrie. The Stone Lion was the first and many more followed, upwards to eleven. Becky's sister, Mona, came up with a new moniker for Guthrie as "The Bed and Breakfast Capital of Oklahoma," and together they muddled through the red tape to make it official. It became Guthrie's new title in 1995, and while most people point to Becky as the one that got it done, she's adamant when she says, "It was Mona's idea. She's the one that deserves the credit."

Over the years, Becky Luker had been accused of some unusual practices, but she was reluctant to embrace the ghostly activity of the old Houghton mansion. The ambiance was prime with the popularity of the mystery dinner theater, the old embalming table, which had been moved out into the main hall, and a visit to a cemetery as a feature of one of the mysteries. Paranormal groups started wanting to investigate the house for ghosts, which seemed unusual to Becky. She doesn't even like calling spirits "ghosts," preferring to say that they are, "something that remains that hasn't moved on."

Stories continued to mount as employees reported other odd activity such as a man in a top hat being seen in the mirror of The Parlor suite and figures and shadows spotted in the basement. The Stone Lion Inn had already developed quite a reputation before the *Ghost Hunters* crew, with The Atlantic Paranormal Society (TAPS) and Oklahoma Paranormal Research and Investigations (OKPRI), showed up in 2006.

OKPRI's previous investigations had already revealed many interesting occurrences, including light anomalies recorded in The Parlor suite, doors slamming on their own, and an audible voice that said, "Get out," in the Kentucky Daisy suite, which was also picked up on an audio recorder.

The investigation with TAPS netted a number of other strange events. Grant Wilson and Christy Clark caught high electromagnetic field (EMF) readings in the Kentucky Daisy suite. It's believed that random high EMF readings could mean that there is some paranormal activity present. Later on, they saw shadows moving around in the Wedding suite, picked up some more high EMF readings, and they both heard Grant's name uttered by a disembodied voice although it wasn't picked up on the audio recorder. Using a thermal imaging camera, Jason Hawes discovered an odd heat signature on a pillow in The Parlor suite, as if only a head had been lying on the bed. He tested what the signature would look like if an entire body had been on the bed, and the heat signature covered the entire bed, not just the pillow. In the middle of the basement, Dave Tango felt what he described as a "web" pulling through his arm. Also in the basement, Jason and Grant caught an electronic voice phenomenon (EVP) that sounded like a child's voice saying, "Can you find me? Find me."

As of this writing, I've twice been to The Stone Lion Inn. The first time my wife and I treated her brother and sister-in-law to the murder mystery dinner theater for his birthday. We had an absolutely fantastic time trying to solve a nicely twisted mystery (our team did manage to solve it correctly), met some wonderful people, and enjoyed exploring the classic mansion. While there were footsteps emanating from the third floor throughout the night, most of the action happened the following morning.

The ghosts of The Stone Lion Inn like to play with electronics. Perhaps it's because they didn't have those types of gadgets in their day or they're just being playful in general. One of our guest mates kept powering off his cell phone because he didn't want to take any calls that morning. Much to his chagrin, it kept turning back on. I had brought an audio recorder with me and left it on in the hallway throughout the night to try and capture whatever ghostly voices I could. When I packed it away, even though I had the device set to the "hold" position, which prevents any pressed buttons from functioning, the audio recorder began playing.

The embalming table is used to serve drinks right next to the impressive staircase.

Not long after, a group of guests who hadn't ventured around the mansion the night before traversed the stairs to the third floor playroom. Once up there, they thought they heard footsteps on the stairs although no one else was coming up. A moment later, my wife saw a shadow dart from the open door to our room, the Lucille Mulhall Suite, and into the bathroom. I stepped into the bathroom and found no one there.

My second foray to The Stone Lion Inn was during a paranormal investigation with OKPRI, which I included a bit of at the beginning of this tale. It was quite an active night for the house, and it started in the entrance hall on the first floor. There's a bureau that rests there blocking the main double doors to what had been the parlor and is now The Parlor suite. For some odd reason one of the top drawers had been open and it suddenly slammed shut as we gathered near the small hall that now takes you to The Parlor's suite entrance. One of our investigators, Johnny Longan, was using a Tri-Field EMF detector at the time and I took a snapshot of him using it over by the bureau. There's an interesting white wisp between him and the bureau in the photograph.

A while later, I was in the library across the entrance hall sweeping the room with a K-II meter, another type of EMF detector that uses a series of colored lights from green to red that signal strength. The K-II was keeping relatively quiet when, suddenly, it started spiking high into the red near the fireplace. At the same time, I felt a surge of energy hit me full on from the front and I got light-headed. Then, as quickly as it had come, it was gone.

A white wisp floats between Johnny Longan and the bureau in the foyer.

The staircase was quite an adventure for us that night. As described above, a group of us were headed up the stairs when the door to one of the suites creaked open. Much to my amusement, it turned out to be the door to the Lucille Mulhall suite where my wife and I had stayed just weeks earlier. However, earlier that evening, we had a bit more of a scare. I was climbing the staircase and was about halfway up when one of our other investigators started to set forth upward. We both jumped when a framed photograph on the wall between us suddenly fell off and shattered across the stairs. When we caught our breath, we noticed it was Becky's personalized photograph of Lizzie Borden, the infamous New England spinster who was accused of hatcheting her parents to death in 1892.

The Stone Lion Inn could very well be one of the most haunted houses in Oklahoma. At times, Becky Luker has been accused of staging some of her hauntings, but from personal experience I'd have to say those accusations are absolutely false. Anyone looking for some murder mystery fun in a real haunted house for a birthday, anniversary, or any occasion whatsoever, should definitely spend a night at the Stone Lion Inn. You never know what may await you.

Part 2

Oklahoma City

Chapter Seven
Overholser Mansion

The word extravagant should be considered a light term when describing the Overholser Mansion. Just the carriage house alone is 4,000 square feet — enough to house a few modern day families. And the mansion? Well, standing at more than 11,000 square feet, it is ornate in architecture, lavishly furnished with an interior of Antwerp Oak, and accoutered with stain glass windows. Built in 1903, this was the home of Henry Overholser, his wife, Anna, and their family.

Henry Overholser was an integral part of Oklahoma City's early development. He was born in Ohio in 1846 and, after many successful business ventures in Indiana, Colorado, and Wisconsin, he arrived in Oklahoma to make a larger fortune from the Land Run of 1889 into the Unassigned Lands. He had purchased prefabricated wooden buildings from Michigan and had them delivered just before his arrival in current day Oklahoma City.

The beautiful Overholser Mansion had renovation work done in 2010.

Overholser immediately set to work on erecting a half dozen buildings on land he had purchased on what is now Sheridan Avenue. The forethought earned him instant credibility in the business community, and within a month he was elected president of the new Board of Trade (now the Chamber of Commerce).

Overholser continued to drive business to Oklahoma City. After the basic city was established, he brought in services and entertainment by constructing the Grand Avenue Hotel in 1889 and the Overholser Theater in 1890. In 1895, he partnered with C. G. Jones to connect Oklahoma City to Tulsa, Kansas City, and St. Louis via their newly formed St. Louis and Oklahoma City Railroad; service began operating in 1897 on the Frisco line. While this was being developed, Overholser also worked on bringing a streetcar system to the city. In 1906, he assisted the Chamber of Commerce in purchasing land for the State Fair of Oklahoma, another testament to how he was involved in nearly all aspects of Oklahoma City's growth until he sadly passed away in 1915.

Henry Overholser had arrived in Oklahoma with a son and daughter from a previous marriage, which had ended in divorce nine years before. Within six months of arriving for the land run, Henry married Anna Ione Murphy, daughter of Oklahoma's first territorial treasurer, and together they had a son and daughter. Unfortunately, their son passed away shortly after childbirth. Overholser's son from his first marriage, Edward, later became mayor of Oklahoma City.

Henry and Anna's daughter, Henry (yes, a daughter named Henry), married David Perry in 1926, and together they lived with Anna at Overholser Mansion in Classen's Highland Park Addition, now known as Heritage Hills. Anna passed ownership over to her daughter in 1937, prior to her death in 1940, and, since the Perry's had no children, the property ended up in the hands of David Perry after his wife passed away in 1959.

The Oklahoma Chapter of American Institute of Architects, Historical Preservation Incorporated, and private citizens raised the money to purchase Overholser Mansion and its furnishings from an aging David Perry in 1972. After the acquisition, the property was donated to the State of Oklahoma. Today, the Oklahoma Historical Society manages it in partnership with Preservation Oklahoma.

The ghosts of the Overholser Mansion are said to be that of the family, concerned about its present-day condition even though it is kept relatively close to its state from the early 1900s. Docents that work at the mansion report activity mainly occurs in specific areas, such as the Nursery, Monroney Bedroom, the Collections Area storage room adjacent to the ballroom, the Parlor where Mr. Overholser's funeral was held, and the North Carriage Stairway. Many of these reports consist of feelings of fear, anticipation, hair standing on the back of the neck, being watched, and queasiness. However, more exciting things happen as well.

Doors close on their own when there's no draft, curtains are pulled back by someone that is not visible, brooms are randomly discovered in the hall, and beds throughout the house are left with impressions as if someone has just sat down there. One docent claims, "The miniature bathtub in the Nursery seems to move forward a little bit at a time. I have never physically witnessed the movement, but it appears to be in a slightly different place each time I enter the room."

Some people have seen the apparition of Anna Overholser — head and body only — floating throughout the house. One witness claims that she saw Anna peering out from one of the third floor windows. Others swear to have seen the opaque body young woman gliding out of the music room on the first floor and cross the hall. This may be a residual haunting because each witness that has seen her has described the young woman's actions in the same fashion.

Chapter Eight

The Skirvin Hotel

Who was Effie? That's been the ongoing mystery at the Skirvin Hotel in downtown Oklahoma City for decades. The local legend is that Effie was a chambermaid who worked at the Skirvin back during its heyday in the early 1900s. She was attractive and the owner, William B. Skirvin, took up with her and they had a child together. He kept her and the baby a secret from his high-powered business associates and set them up with a room on the top floor in exchange for her silence. The legend tells us that depression overcame Effie and she jumped out the window with baby in hand, both of them dying upon impact ten stories below.

The story gained national attention in January 2010 when players of the NBA's New York Knicks blamed their 106-88 thrashing by the Oklahoma City Thunder on the ghosts of the Skirvin. The *New York Daily News* reported that player Eddy Curry stated, "They said it happened on the tenth floor and I'm the only one staying on the tenth floor. That's why I spent most of my time in (Nate Robinson's) room. I definitely believe there are ghosts in that hotel."

With the national coverage, the Skirvin Hotel joined the likes of the Renaissance Vinoy Hotel in St. Petersburg Florida, which has had strange occurrences reported by players of the Boston Red Sox when they're in town to play the Tampa Bay Rays, as an old luxury hotel with a haunted history that spooks high-paid athletes. Two weeks after the report from the Knicks, Taj Gibson of the Chicago Bulls claimed that at 12:15 a.m. his bathroom door at the Skirvin slammed shut on its own. He left the room and spent the rest of the night with a teammate.

The problem with the Effie haunting, however, is that there is no record of her ever having worked at the Skirvin, nor is there any record of her death, which should have garnered some kind of story in the local paper. Even if W. B. Skirvin was able to mask her identity, it's hard to just simply ignore a mother and her baby plummeting ten stories to their deaths. According to Steve Lackmeyer and Steve Money in their book, *Skirvin*, W. B. was a notorious womanizer and drinker, tenth floor salesmen suites were sometimes used as gambling dens, and police occasionally raided the suites finding roulette wheels, loose women, and bullet holes. However, there was no hotel record or document for Effie during their two years of research, and it is believed that Skirvin's bookkeeper and assistant, Mabel Luty, was romantically involved with him. She survived past Skirvin's death in 1945, and she never jumped from any windows.

Is it Effie that haunts the historic Skirvin Hotel, or is it someone else?

All that considered, the haunting of a woman does permeate throughout the building. Guests have reported on numerous occasions a disembodied female voice in their room while staying alone. Others, meanwhile, have sworn the form of a nude woman has joined them in the shower and one man insisted he was sexually assaulted by an invisible entity. A former security guard before the hotel closed in the

1980s even claimed that the female spirit tried to enter his body and produce "feelings" inside him. Couple these incidents with the sound of a ghostly maid's cart being wheeled down the hall when there is none to be found, and the cry of a baby echoing upon the air, and the story of Effie seems to hold a bit of merit. Is her legend a conglomerate of all these hauntings?

They say building renovation stirs up the restless spirits. For more than fifteen years beginning in 1988, the Skirvin Hotel sat dormant, a mere shell of its former self: boarded up, vandalized, a shelter for the homeless, and on the verge of being torn down. During a walk-through in 1999, gang graffiti littered the once elegant walls, broken glass was shattered across the floor, and a gas can was discovered in the ballroom. It was a sad state for a building that had once hosted rich oil barons, presidents, famous generals, and celebrities.

The Skirvin's origins didn't simply begin with construction on an open lot in Oklahoma's vast open plains. Oklahoma City was already a thriving town, and the massive footprint of the hotel meant older buildings were going to have to be removed. This caused a bit of controversy. Similar to today when a historic landmark is threatened with demolition, so too did some of our predecessors become upset. In the case of the Skirvin, not only were buildings removed, but even one they had been trying to preserve, the old Richardson Real Estate Office, crumbled to pieces in the wake of the hotel's construction. One of the first houses to be built in Oklahoma City, it had been standing since 1889.

The Skirvin Hotel opened as a jewel in downtown Oklahoma City in 1911, a ten-story social and political hub with all the glamour of the big city. It was ornate with marbled floors, hand-carved woodwork, and Austrian crystal chandeliers. Theodore Roosevelt stayed there in 1912, and the room he used quickly became known as the "President's Suite." However, it wouldn't be long before a dark cloud hung over the extravagant building.

The hotel's first reported death was a gruesome and controversial one. Frederick W. Scherubel was the managing director and one of the largest stockholders of the Skirvin in 1913 when he was found, gun in hand, shot through the temple in his bathroom at the hotel in Room 314 at 3:30 p.m. on April 10.

The *Daily Oklahoman* newspaper didn't hold back in describing the horrific scene from the viewpoint of Dr. H. H. Gipson:

> "He opened the door and saw Scherubel lying on the floor with his head in a pool of coagulated blood. The legs were doubled under the body. The right arm was underneath the head, and a revolver lying

a few inches from the outstretched hand. Scherubel was alive with a strong pulse showing. The blood from the wounds had coagulated and formed a clot extending from the mass on the floor to the opening in the wounds."

Gipson and Dr. Thomas A. Buchanan moved Scherubel to the bed and examined the extent of the damage. Deducing that there was no hope for the man, they placed him in a more comfortable position, and within forty minutes after he was found, Scherubel died. All looked like the hotel director had taken his life.

The body was taken to Marshall & Harper undertaking, and it was there that the mortician, E. L. Hahn, noticed something peculiar. A bruise appeared on Scherubel's face that had not been there the previous morning. He also discovered that there were no powder marks or burns near the wound, which should have been present if the man had shot himself, and the hair had not been scorched.

The revolver was actually the property of Morris Brown, the assistant manager, and Scherubel had taken it when a few of the Skirvin cooks had caused Scherubel trouble and he wanted to protect himself. No note had been left.

Despite these findings, Fred Scherubel's death was ruled a suicide. He had been suffering from severe problems with his adenoids, underwent several surgeries, and had actually had bone removed from his nose to try and alleviate the pain. He was sleep-deprived, reduced to about two hours of rest each night, and he had recently made the comment that he "didn't see how a man could possibly live through such agony." It was determined that following a polite conversation with Brown, Scherubel entered his room, was overcome with a desire to end the pain, grabbed the revolver from the dresser, sat on a stool in the bathroom, and pulled the trigger.

A Mason, Scherubel's funeral was conducted under the auspices of his Order. Whether his death was truly a suicide or a homicide is still debatable and will likely never be known.

Although there was one other aberration not long after its opening when Sam St. Mary, the renowned local tailor whose shop was just one door north of the Skirvin, killed bagageman W. F. Henry right outside the building in 1917, the Skirvin continued to bask in its grandeur and majesty, and most of the city's popular clubs and associations would hold meetings there. In March 1919, the Skirvin Hotel held what could be called its first paranormal conference. Billed as "spiritualist meetings," the event was headlined by Edna Bacon of Blackwell who gave a lecture about "The Infinite Intelligence." Other discussions covering the philosophy and phenomena of spiritualism were held throughout the two-day event, and messages from spirits of the dead were given through mediums that were present.

General John J. Pershing, commander of the United States forces during World War I, was honored at the Skirvin Hotel on February 10, 1920. In a receiving line to greet the distinguished general was the man who would later become America's last living World War I veteran, Frank Woodruff Buckles.

Lobby.

Main Dining Room.

A vintage postcard depicts the Skirvin in 1920.

It's also said that during prohibition the Skirvin housed a popular speakeasy, and in 1926 one of the African American bellhops were arrested for possession of whiskey.

Renovations in 1930 added a new wing, raised the entire hotel to fourteen levels, and increased capacity to 525 rooms. Totaling $3 million dollars, twice the price of the original hotel construction, a roof garden and cabaret were added, the lobby was doubled in size, new Gothic lanterns suspended from the ceiling were installed, hand-carved English fumed oak was added to the walls and doors, and the café was enlarged and turned into a coffee shop. The rooftop Venetian Room ushered in an era of music and dancing at the Skirvin.

Just afterward, W. B. Skirvin further expanded with a tower annex across the street on Broadway. However, financial problems and the depressed economy forced construction to be halted in 1932, and it wouldn't be picked up again until 1934. It was scaled back to fourteen floors, and few of them were even ready when it was finally opened in 1938. In fact, the final floors weren't leased out until Sohio Petroleum grabbed the top three levels in 1949.

The 1930s were darker days for the Skirvin Hotel. Not only was the tower project a mess, but also the Skirvin family was wrapped up in a major lawsuit between themselves over finances and company holdings. It was exasperating to the point that even federal district judge A. P. Murrah, fists clenched in the courtroom, leaned across the bench and roared at the family that they needed to settle their dispute and make up, adding, "You ought to be ashamed of yourselves."

On October 13, 1932, E. H. Fulton, a salesman from Dallas, leaped out of a tenth floor window to his death below. The jump and the level from which Fulton plunged are certainly reminiscent of the mysterious Effie legend. His room had actually been on the fourth floor, but he walked up the stairs to the tenth, opened a window on the stairway, and hurled himself out. He left a note stating, "sorry to cause all this trouble," and his suicide was, "the only way out." He also attached a parking lot check, business cards, instructions to dispose of his personal belongings, and added in the note, "My relatives have no money so please do not worry them."

The first governor of Oklahoma, Charles Nathaniel Haskell, lived in a suite at the Skirvin Hotel, and it was there that he succumbed to pneumonia on July 5, 1933. He had first become ill in March of that year when he collapsed in the hotel lobby. Reportedly, he was making a gradual improvement until the day prior to his death.

In another incident reminiscent of Effie, a twenty-year-old woman from Nashville, Tennessee, nearly dove out of her eighth floor window in August 1939. Following up on a disturbance complaint, house officer Sam Miles entered the room just in time to witness the drunken girl leaping out the window head first. He caught her feet just in time and pulled her back into the room.

The death of William B. Skirvin in 1944 marked the end of an era. His son, O. W. Skirvin sold the hotel to Dan James of the James Hotel Company the following year, and the Skirvin family carried on in other ventures. In fact, W. B.'s daughter, Pearl Skirvin Mesta, went on to become the U.S. Minister to Luxembourg in 1949.

James put into action a ten-year modernization plan, refinishing the suites, remodeling the meeting rooms and clubs, and adding a number of services like a stenographer and notary, a barbershop, and a house physician. In 1948, both Harry Truman and Dwight D. Eisenhower visited the Skirvin. This initiative carried on into the 1950s as a swimming pool was added as well as the Four Seasons Lounge next to the pool. However, by the time the 1960s hit, suburban shopping malls were drawing interest away from downtown and modern transportation was creating congestion in Oklahoma City, so James sold the hotel in 1963.

This began an era of short-lived ownerships with the hotel changing hands in 1968, 1971, 1977, 1979, 1985, and 1987. Finally, in October 1988, the ownership group of Peter Streit and Michael Proffitt abruptly closed the doors of the Skirvin without any advance notice in order to give the interior a $1.5 million renovation and planned to reopen on April 1, 1989. The renovation never happened.

Again, the Skirvin underwent a number of ownership changes, but the doors remained closed and the hotel fell into disrepair. The most notorious of these was by Oesman Sapta, of the Indonesian BYOC International, Inc., who was accused by his partner William Myles of over-financing the Skirvin renovations in order to divert excess funds overseas. A local car dealership that Sapta owned also went belly-up, and BYOC filed for bankruptcy a year later in 1996. Throughout the 1990s, the Skirvin Hotel was placed on the list of endangered historic places, as the building continued to deteriorate and no owner seemed able to figure out how to finance the increasingly expensive renovation needed. Some people called for its demolition while a Native American group proposed turning it into a casino. Finally, in 2003, after the city had acquired the property, a Dallas-based group, promising to spend more than $42 million to renovate the structure and turn it into a Hilton, was designated the winning bidder to develop the Skirvin. It reopened in 2007.

Whether the depressed, yet flirtatious Effie truly exists is likely irrelevant. There is certainly something paranormal going on at the Skirvin Hotel and there is plenty of history from which to draw. Other, less colorful deaths have occurred there as well such as former Enid mayor John Milton Carr in 1939 and Mrs. Minnie Ida Wells in 1953, both of whom died of natural causes in their respective suites. Also, not all of the hauntings at the hotel are Effie-related, and any one of them could be someone else tied to the historic structure.

Guests have felt taps on the shoulder from an unseen hand on the fifth floor. Depending on where you're at in the hotel the scent of perfume or cigar smoke may mysteriously waft up in the air from unknown origins. Some have even seen an African American man dressed in an old hotel uniform, complete with hat and gloves, walk up to the front doors of the hotel and then simply vanish. The man could be any number of former employees from the hotel.

Construction workers renovating the hotel had tools moved out of reach from them and some of the tools just completely vanished. One worker spotted a man in a tailored suit roaming around the fourth floor and was worried that the man wasn't protected from the rampant asbestos. He turned for a moment and when he turned back the man had disappeared. None of the other workers recalled seeing this person. A number of locals claim that William B. Skirvin still roams the halls of the hotel that bears his name and in which he lived. Could he be the mysterious businessman?

Jared Jeffries of the New York Knicks said of the Skirvin's ghosts, "I definitely believe it. The place is haunted. It's scary."

Chapter Nine

Belle Isle

The wind whipped about her, so fast, so hard; the breath was ripped straight out of her chest. She frantically groped at the nothingness before her, arms flailing in the cold, bleak darkness. Just a moment ago she'd been relatively secure, prodding about the grim iron works, but without a light source the last anyone heard of her was a scream that faded away into the depths below. Thus, in the bowels of the decrepit Belle Isle power plant, three floors down from whence she came, ended the life of a twelve year-old girl, extinguished before it had really begun.

When the denizens of the Belle Isle area whisper about the strange occurrences in the area, it is her vestige that is most often called upon. Perhaps this is because hers was the most recent death there, or the most tragic in a life so young and a death so gruesome. However, there is much more to the tale of Belle Isle Station.

Over one hundred years ago in 1907, the Oklahoma Railway Co. broke ground at Belle Isle Lake to build an electric plant that would generate power for its new streetcar network. An ominous sign was cast over the area when at Halloween 1908, a worker at the railway's quarry suffered critical injuries from falling rock as a result of defective machinery. Now, years after the demise and demolition of the power plant, the specters of Belle Isle Station still generate a buzz in the Oklahoma City area.

For a time, Belle Isle was the place to be. Prior to World War I, hoping to attract more people to use the system, Oklahoma Railway invested in the property by adding a park and bathhouses for swimming, and in 1922, an amusement park, complete with a classic carousel and roller coaster, was built, prompting Belle Isle to be dubbed "Oklahoma's Coney Island." Bands, orchestras, and cabarets could be heard nightly, and L. E. Buttrick of the Buttrick School of Dancing added a pavilion to promote the art and the school. Canoe rides for the lake were established and a boardwalk and "Honey Moon Bridge" were added for young lovers. A small zoo existed there once, and it included such animals as deer, bears, and tigers. Belle Isle gained enough popularity to attract the legendary Harry Houdini, who performed one of his famous escapes by being chained up inside of a box and dumped into the lake.

Belle Isle and Bathing Pool.

One of the long forgotten amenities of Belle Isle back in 1920.

Unfortunately, the fun and games at Belle Isle were short-lived. In 1928, Oklahoma Railway sold the power plant, park, and lake to Oklahoma Gas and Electric who promptly closed the majority of the amusement park and built a new state-of-the-art plant with a touch of elegance in its brick design. Many of the rides were sold to Springlake Park, including the carousel, but OG&E kept the remaining park around the lake open for picnics and stocked the lake with fish for recreational fishing for a number of years. Eventually, in 1953, that access was also revoked.

In 1961, the small plant built by Oklahoma Railway was demolished and the functionality of the OG&E plant began to decrease. By 1980, the plant completely closed and it remained dormant for nearly twenty years until it was finally destroyed and replaced by a retail shopping center.

Riddled throughout its history, even during the years that Belle Isle was a recreational hotspot, the location met with a number of tragedies. Less than four years after the quarry accident, a nineteen-year-old Texas boy drowned when a boat in which he and a friend were paddling overturned in Belle Isle Lake. During the summer of 1926, Mrs. L. W. Elmore lost her hat on the amusement park's roller coaster, reached for it, and was struck by a beam at the side of the track. She fell eight feet. When she was found, it was discovered that she had fractured her skull and the upper part of her body was crushed.

Of interesting note during that time, Rose Hill Cemetery would place ads in the Oklahoma boasting about how it overlooked Belle Isle Lake. At midnight on May 3, 1924, a "strange light" was seen hovering over the area. According to the account in *The Daily Oklahoman*, "At midnight the strange light appeared to be about 1,000 feet high and hanging over Belle Isle... If it was a balloon light, you couldn't see the balloon. If it was a floating star, it was ten times the size of the ordinary twinkler and had more of a fiery color than other stars."

Fishing-related accidents at Belle Isle Lake became a staple in the 1930s, and some of these also resulted in the loss of life. One such man suffered a heart attack while fishing at the water's edge in 1932. Another fell from his boat in 1934, was found struggling in the water, but was unable to be revived after being brought ashore. Although they were not fishing, two teenagers and a man overturned their boat during a church picnic in 1938 when the youths decided to switch places. The two teens were saved, but Ollie Beesley drowned in ten feet of water two hundred feet from the shore while trying to help one of the kids.

The following summer's incidents were more mischievous. Local teenagers had taken to shooting the insulators from OG&E's equipment. They would gather near the power plant with rifles and pistols and would shoot the glass insulators for target practice. The kids enjoyed the tinkling shatter of the glass.

However, for the next fifty years, incidents around the Belle Isle plant simmered down as the park was finally closed and it was simply a power plant humming away by the waterside...until it was finally closed in 1980. From that time forward, vandals and adventurous teens broke into the building, even though steel sheeting had been applied over many of the doors and windows on the first two levels, and there were even rumors that a satanic cult had used the plant's water intake system to house alligators. The entire building fell into disrepair and became a danger zone.

On October 5, 1990, an article ran in *The Daily Oklahoman* describing the plant's inevitable date with doom, although it had not yet been determined. It also stated that while the building had been re-secured two or three years prior, doorplates had been pulled off, allowing access to anyone who neared. There was a bit of a squabble over who should secure it again — the city had contacted the Federal Deposit Insurance Corp. (FDIC) who owned it, but if the FDIC didn't secure it then a contractor was going to have to be brought in. Just three weeks later, at Halloween as it had eighty-two years prior, death manifested at Belle Isle.

An artist's depiction of the Belle Isle power plant.
Courtesy of Collin Ricksecker.

Randall Dickerson had been shooting the breeze and having a few drinks with three friends at the old power plant on a brisk autumn evening. At 5:30 p.m. Randall's friend's left, but Randall decided to stay at Belle Isle and he ventured inside the brick hulk. About five hours later that night, a group of four teens snuck inside to explore the crumbling structure, but scrambled out when they found Randall Dickerson sprawled out on the floor in a pool of his own blood. Authorities later determined that Dickerson plummeted from a beam some five stories from above the ground.

Nearly four and a half years later, on January 6, 1995, twelve-year-old Tia Jones met the same fate from a height of three stories. Without a flashlight, she fell through a gap in the flooring she and her friends had not seen.

The shrunken lake of Belle Isle, where so many had died in the
early twentieth century, viewed from the back of a strip mall.

The building was a death trap, but even with all the known dangers, during any given season as many as 150 arrests would be made of trespassers that would break into the property. Amongst them were ghost-hunting groups that had heard rumors of the spirits of Belle Isle's dead. Tales at the time talked about sloshing noises emanating from the floor, as if someone that had just come out of the water was walking through the facility, but no one could be seen. Another was that of a ghostly girl pacing back and forth and looking out from four of the third floor windows.

The Belle Isle power plant did not want to go willingly on that bitter January morning in 1999. Originally estimated to implode in ten seconds, extra explosives were brought in after a first round failed to complete the task. In the end, the remaining structure needed to be shoved over.

In its place was built a retail shopping center. However, while the structure of the Belle Isle power plant may be gone and the lake a faint remnant of its former glory, the energy of its past still remains.

During construction of the shopping center, a number of the workers had strange experiences with machines operating oddly...and some even started operating on their own. For a time they thought it was local teens coming in and playing around with the equipment, but no teens were ever discovered.

One particular retailer has had employees heard their names called after-hours and loud bangs emanate from the back wall of the store at times. At another establishment it's been quite commonplace that when the store is opened up in the morning items for sale on the front tables have been knocked off. Odd cold spots are felt throughout a number of different stores in the shopping center and sometimes a ghostly mist rolls in at night.

The history behind Belle Isle Station is tragic, yet most customers who frequent the stores shopping for shoes, clothes, and any number of other items are completely unaware of what happened upon the soil and in the water of which they pass. The railcars, amusement park, and power plant are long since gone, but the memories and energy still remain through the historic grounds.

Chapter Ten

The Purple Church

Located just east of the limits of Oklahoma City, near Spencer, "The Purple Church" remains shrouded in mystery. The ruins are simply that of a foundation and its cellar, the rest of the building having been burned away long ago, and there is nothing purple about the remains tucked way back in the woods. It's believed that it was titled "The Purple Church" because of a few purple pentagrams that were spray painted in the basement area. No matter what the color of the foundation may be, tales of the paranormal and the occult have flowed out of the location for years.

The cellar rests on private property, but for years groups have ventured back there and performed dark rituals before being chased off. Some people that have made the trek report that they have seen evidence of animal sacrifices. It is even rumored that the mid-1980s murder and professed Satanist Sean Sellers practiced his rituals at the Purple Church before killing a Circle K clerk, his mother, and his father, and claiming demonic possession.

The site has become more of a dare location for teens and college students, testing their nerves and seeing if the rumors are true that someone will chase them down with a shotgun if they go near. However, the occasional paranormal team will make it back into the woods to check out the old cellar. Bones, a broken bench, and graffiti are the trademark of the location, but unexplainable floating lights have been seen as well. Disembodied voices fade in and out and sometimes screams are heard. Shadows lurk throughout the rooms of the cellar, and there have been reports of glowing red eyes hovering in a dark corner.

What really happens there is still speculation and lore. Whether Satanic cults really go there to worship or whether it's an actively haunted cellar can be debated, but one thing is for certain: The Purple Church is very creepy.

Deep within the brush past the curve in this road are the ruins known as "The Purple Church."

Chapter Eleven

Puckett's Ghost

Not all local legends are a century or more old. As time goes by, new ones are introduced into the fabric of our society and continue to shape our culture. The controversy of Puckett's Ghost is one such legend that has emerged in recent years, and is the subject of much debate in the Oklahoma City area after its excessive media exposure.

On September 12, 2002, Oklahoma's News Channel 4 broadcast a surveillance video from Puckett's wrecker service, which showed the apparition of a woman floating through the lot and straight through old vehicles. The apparition was first noticed by Puckett's employee Kathy Henley, who had been watching the surveillance camera at the time and noticed something odd float across the screen. The crew at Puckett's was sure they had caught a rare ghost on film and contacted the media.

The family of Tracy Martin, a 33-year-old mother with twins who had recently died in a car accident, came forward and believed the apparition to look like her. Tracy's car had, in fact, been moved to Puckett's that past July. Investigators believe her accident would not have been fatal had she been wearing her seat belt.

The video has made the rounds on the Internet and can be viewed on any number of popular websites. This has only fueled the debate of validity. Rocky Mountain Paranormal Group claims they have recreated the video effect "Pepper's Ghost" with a camera, G. I. Joe action figure, string, flashlight, and Plexiglas, demonstrating how those objects could have been used to create such a clip as the one from Puckett's. They posted their recreation video online, but others have scoffed at the debunking of the apparition, and the two polarizing sides remain entrenched.

While the location is eerie at night, aside from this surveillance video, there have been no other claims of paranormal activity at Puckett's.

Do some ghosts haunt their old abandoned or wrecked cars?

Part 3

Northeast Oklahoma

Chapter Twelve

Legends of the 101 Ranch

A national historic landmark, the Miller Brothers 101 Ranch was an 110,000-acre ranch that was the headquarters of one of the most famous Wild West shows of the early 1900s. In 1903, Colonel George W. Miller left this massive ranch to his three sons Joe, George, and Zach. During its prosperous early development, the ranch was expanded via land run and securing leases with the Ponca Indian Tribe as it stretched across Noble, Pawnee, Osage, and Kay counties. The Miller brothers raised herds of Holstein, Shorthorn, and Hereford dairy cattle in addition to Duroc-Jersey hogs. Their numerous facilities surrounding their famed "White House" headquarters included a packing plant, ice plant, tannery, dairy, cannery, general store, café, and hotel, as well as other buildings and innovations of the era like their own telephone system. However, it was their Wild West show that netted them fame.

A poster of the 101 Ranch's famous Wild West show. *Courtesy of the 101 Ranch Old Timers' Association.*

In an agreement with the National Editorial Association of St. Louis, the Millers held a massive Wild West extravaganza at the 101 Ranch while the association held its annual convention in Guthrie in June 1905. It was a resounding success as more than 65,000 people attended. The events included parades, roping events, buffalo chases, and cowboy and Indian reenactments. Wild West show legends like Bill Pickett and Lucille Mulhall attended and performed their many tricks. Permission was granted by the United States government to release the infamous Apache Geronimo, then a prisoner of war at Fort Sill, to participate in the events with other Indian chiefs from around the region. The Millers even offered $1,000 to anyone that would volunteer to be scalped by Geronimo.

With the success of the event, the show hit the road in 1907 at the Jamestown Exposition in Virginia, and the touring days of the 101 Ranch Wild West Show began. Seven years later they actually purchased a Mexican army, including livestock, wagons, and weapons. They sold some of this back to the Mexican government, used a bit for the show, and some they used on the ranch, including a Gatling gun they mounted on top of one of the silos. The Wild West Show also began performing internationally at this time. Although their initial trip to England cost them their horses, stagecoaches, and automobiles for the brewing war effort, this was redeemed in 1925 when the show performed for the King and Queen of England and 700,000 spectators over the course of thirty-three shows.

The Millers believed that their Wild West show was preserving a piece of American culture. Zach T. Miller stated in 1908:

"That the American cowboy is passing, slowley [sic], but irredeemably passing, is a saddening, but incontrovertible fact. A more picturesque and daring, yet a more kind hearted and gentle class of men never existed in any section at any time." He continued, "The cowboy's disappearance is such as to occasion the manly to weep, the lover of the rugged, the pure, the noble to cry for a return of the days that were. But supplications, hopes and regrets are alike in vain, for a condition of American life is on the march to glorified extinction, and will never be recreated."

The 101 Ranch is credited with a number of successful agricultural developments, coining the term "cowgirl," and they formed the 101 Ranch Bison Film Company which shot some of the earliest western movies. In 1932, however, just a few years after brothers Joe and George passed away and not unlike many other businesses of the day, Zach and the 101 Ranch went bankrupt.

One of the stranger tales associated with the 101 Ranch is that of Kansas's special law officer George C. Montgomery. Someone fired a shotgun blast through his sitting room window as he was filling out reports for the Santa Fe Railway, killing him. The murderer has never been identified. Montgomery had made a few enemies in Oklahoma in 1901 when one of the Santa Fe trains heading southbound was "robbed" in the state and caused the arrest of Zach Miller and Bill Potts, one of the 101 ranch hands, by Montgomery. The case went to trial in Perry, but it was revealed that there was a misunderstanding with the train conductor about a shipment of cattle. There had been no agent on the train that day to receive the check for payment and the conductor wanted cash for the delivery of the cattle. At first, George Miller cut him a check anyway and the conductor was going to respond by taking the cattle on to Arkansas City, but he then agreed to wait for the arrival of Joe Miller with the required cash. There were no pistols drawn, and the conductor had been properly paid, although the train was off its schedule.

However, there were words exchanged between George Montgomery and Joe while in Perry. Miller and the officer entered a tense discussion, but Montgomery didn't respond to the final insult until Joe turned away. It was then that Montgomery punched Miller from behind, and Joe responded by pulling a small knife. Montgomery ran for the door.

O. W. Coffelt of the 101 Ranch was eventually charged in the murder of George C. Montgomery. Montgomery's fellow officers had always believed there was a conspiracy by the Millers, and they had hired someone to take care of him. A witness had put Coffelt in Winfield, Montgomery's hometown, on the day of the murder, but there was no substantial evidence and the local sheriff had been out to the 101 Ranch that morning and reportedly found everyone properly at home. Coffelt was tried and acquitted four times for the crime.

The classic landmark "White House" of the 101 Ranch, also known as the "Palace on the Oklahoma Prairie," was actually the third structure used as a home and headquarters for the Miller family. When Colonel George W. Miller and his son, Joe, negotiated a land deal with the Ponca Indians in 1892, they built a dugout house of lumber and a sod roof as well as an adjacent corral that remained in operation until after the Colonel's death in 1903. In fact, the patriarch of the family never saw the home he was building completed since the official sale of the acreage was delayed for years, and the Miller's were not allowed to build permanent improvements to the land until they properly acquired the title. Colonel Miller died in the sod headquarters on April 15, 1903, after a battle with pneumonia. Many Ponca Indians, including Chief White Eagle, paid their respects to Colonel Miller at the home.

After the passing of George W. Miller, the family completed building the home as quickly as they could, sold their home in Kansas, and ate their first meal at the new residence on Christmas Day in 1903. Styled like a plantation home, it was considered one of the finest houses in Oklahoma, and had been so anticipated that the first major social event it held happened prior to its completion on October 31, 1903, when only daughter Alma married attorney William Henry England.

Unfortunately, not even six years later, a fire burst out from the basement of the house in the middle of the night on January 14, 1909, and the family barely escaped with their lives. Tragically, the family dog,

The majesty of the famous 101 white house back in its heyday.
Courtesy of the 101 Ranch Old Timers' Association.

"Little Sol," perished in the blaze, but only after heroically waking his master, George L., who was sound asleep. The cause of the fire is still a mystery to this day.

The family decided to build an even more lavish house atop the site of their former home, and this is what has come to be known as the White House. The November 1926 issue the *Rock Island Magazine* described the mansion as, "Entering the spacious living room furnished in exquisite taste, polished floors given color by rare rugs, woven by the Indians, walls adorned with paintings a connoisseur might envy, one is impressed with the feeling of harmony of thought and the realization of ideals. Each piece of furniture is placed to the best advantage and is well chosen for such a home. There is nothing that is not needed, yet beauty is everywhere."

All that remains of the great white house of the 101.

The ruins of the White House seem to be the most paranormally active location on the property. Sadly, all that remains is a foundation and the floor of the first level. After the government possessed the estate following the Miller bankruptcy, they stripped down the interior of the house and sold off the contents at salvage value. Following that, the Farm Security Administration ordered the building's demolition, which was partly a health hazard from the asbestos roof that had been added to prevent another fire. Presently, visitors are not permitted to walk on the remnants of the first floor due to instability of the structure, but those allowed to investigate the property are able to venture into the crumbling basement.

When one first walks in to this basement, there is a room directly straight ahead on the opposite side of the staircase that is rather lively with activity. There is no electricity whatsoever near the building, but K-II meters and gaussmeters happily spike without explanation. Investigators have felt touched and poked in the small room, and psychics have picked up on spirits still living in the remnants of the home. During a joint investigation between OKPRI and SPIES Extreme Paranormal, psychic Christy Clark picked up on one hospitable woman who offered the group a place to sleep with fresh linen in rooms that haven't existed in decades.

Inside the ruins of the white house where a spirit wished to prepare us rooms to spend the night.

Tragedy engulfed the Miller family in the later years of the 101. When Joe married his second wife in 1926, she didn't want to live in the great white family home, so they lived in a separate house a few miles down the road. Joe was found dead there October 21, 1927, in the garage after inhaling too much carbon monoxide. His car had been giving him problems at the time and he was seemingly working on it when he died. The hood of the car was up, the garage door was partly open, and a few screws had been removed from the motor. At some point he inhaled too many of the dangerous fumes and succumbed, collapsing to the floor. Joe's house still stands there, dilapidated now and disintegrating. Windows are broken, floors have fallen through to the basement, and the roof is caving in. However, the spirit of Joe and, perhaps, someone else lingers there. The form of a woman has been seen standing outside of the garage. Is it Miller's wife, Mary, still mourning over the loss of the husband she'd only had for a year? Inside, something bangs on the broken and fallen boards, whispers, and expels energy at people who won't leave and let it be.

Joe wasn't the only brother who had car problems. On February 1, 1929, George L. Miller, the "financial wizard" of the family had been returning from oil negotiations in Texas in sleet and blizzard-like conditions. He had already made it back to Ponca City for business, and started heading home at about midnight. George L. hit a slick patch of ice on the road and crashed. It appeared he tried to jump out, but failed to jump far enough to safety. He was found pinned under one of the wheels of the car two hours after the accident. Barely alive, George was rushed to the hospital in Ponca City, but he died before he got there.

Colonel George W. Miller had raised his sons to each have strong, unique abilities so that together the three of them could build a successful ranch. Joe was the farmer and also kept operations organized at the ranch. George was the financier and managed the family's oil interests. Zach's expertise was as the cowman and managing the cattle of the ranch; he also served as the President of the Cherokee Strip Cowpunchers Association. With Joe's organizational skills and George L.'s financial brains lost, the burden became insurmountable for Zach when the Great Depression hit.

Almost overnight the oil business plummeted, wheat, corn, and hogs were almost worthless, and cattle sold at their lowest figure. Operations at the 101 Ranch came to a halt and the Wild West Show was left stranded in Washington D.C. in August 1931. Zach desperately tried to keep the ranch afloat, calling a conference of his creditors at the 101 White House that month and asking for six months to get reorganized. They were willing to work with him and save the traditions of the ranch, but the lawsuits and threats of federal receivership needed to stop in order for him to pull the money together. This was assured him, but just weeks later a claim of receivership was filed marking the beginning of the end.

A general operating receiver, Fred C. Clarke, was designated on September 16, 1931, but he soon abandoned any plan of restoring the 101 Ranch as he originally stated he would. Instead, he leased out portions of the land to individual farmers and sold off personal property of the ranch, including remaining livestock, feed, saddles and harnesses, and farm equipment. All that was spared was the White House and its furnishings. Zach declared it "legal robbery" and fired his six-shooter and later a shotgun to try and stop the sales. A year after he was appointed, Clarke was ousted from his position; however, the damage had been done. He was charged with grossly neglecting the ranch, not cultivating the land, and allowing buildings to fall into ruin.

Management was returned to Zach Miller, but finances had grown worse under Clarke, and Zach was left to manage the disintegration of the 101. While he fought hard to keep the land together, he needed to start auctioning it off just to pay the mortgage. He kept hold of the White House, but the 110,000 acres that surrounded it quickly dwindled down to one. Foreclosure proceedings had claimed the land around the family house, but Zach refused to leave until an injunction was finally filed against him on June 3, 1936. In a last gasp effort, he filed an appeal bond, using the proceeds of an auction of the house furnishings as proceeds. It was denied.

As people gathered for the auction, the local newspaper recounted, "Grim, gray-haired Zach T. Miller stood in the shadows of the old white house Saturday and watched the last of his vast empire crumble under the hammer of an auctioneer."

Understandably, Zach was bitter — and prepared to make a final stand. He exclaimed, "I'm going to stay here and fight until the last dog is dead — or run out of court. This has been my home for fifty years!" However, a deputy marshal was there to make sure Zach left the home.

Alice Lee, who traveled with the Wild West Show and performed shooting and riding tricks, remarked, "I've been here since 1908. I traveled all over the world with the show. They ought to put me up there with the rest of the relics."

A set of dishes the family had bought for $200 sold for $1.00. Zach retorted, "Pass it! If I'm going to give it away, I'll give it to my old Indian friends. Some of them never had any dishes."

The first breach-loading gun brought into the United States went for 50 cents. A famous buffalo painting that sold for $85 had once had a $1,200 offer for it spurned by Joe years prior. Countless antiques, rugs, buffalo robes, guns, and Indian relics were sold for pennies on the dollar.

When the auction was finally over, the article continued, "The last of three famous sons of a famous father stood on the steps of the big white mansion, and gazed over what once was a 110,000-acre ranch. ... Miller looked at deserted, fallen farm buildings that once housed the state's finest blooded cattle and hogs. He looked over weeds and disorder where once were showplace orchids, wheat fields, packing houses, and power plants.

Miller walked slowly down the steps to the car of his sister, Mrs. Alma England, and drove toward Ponca City."

Today, the small historic site is maintained by the 101 Ranch Old Timers Association. Following the release of Michael Wallis's book, *The Real Wild West: The 101 Ranch and the Creation of the American West*, a ceremony was held at the location. Vice President of the Association, Al Ritter, described the proceedings:

"As a safeguard against the rumored presence of 'Evil Spirits', our association retained the services of Pawnee medicine man Kenneth Good Eagle to bless author Michael Wallis, his new book and the 101 Ranch. A ceremony was conducted involving a traditional blessing of burning cedar in an abalone shell and sending the smoke with prayers skyward with an eagle feather as a traditional Native American method of communicating with the 'Great Spirit.' Since then nothing of an evil nature has befell our organization or its holding of all that is left of the once, 'Fabulous Empire'."

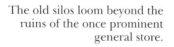

The old silos loom beyond the ruins of the once prominent general store.

Chapter Thirteen

Constantine Theater

Located in downtown Pawhuska, the Constantine Theater was originally built as the Pawhuska House Hotel in 1894, but in 1911 C. A. Constantine purchased the establishment with the intent of transforming it into the finest opera house in the Southwest. Mr. Constantine, born in Constantinople in 1866, began his business ventures in Oklahoma by buying a few cheap lots in Pawhuska in 1906 and renting them out as a bakeshop and a confectionery. These shops proved successful, so he expanded his operations, and by the time he became interested in establishing the theater he had also added candy and ice cream manufacturing to his list of successful businesses.

The Constantine Theater was completed in 1914 and, at the time, was considered the finest establishment of its kind in the state while also boasting Oklahoma's second largest stage. The heating, ventilation, and lighting were of the most current design, and the seating was built for comfort, using chairs six inches wider than standard theaters of the day. Constantine also established a café that adjoined the theater.

While Mr. Constantine ran his business for a profit, offering a variety of dramatic presentations and motion pictures, he also frequently opened the theater's doors to school commencements and religious assemblies. He was a 32-degree Mason of the Scottish Rite, affiliated with the Benevolent and Protective Order of the Elks, and a member of the Knights of Pythias. These organizations also had access to his stage. Additionally, his youngest daughter, Antigone, may have been inspired by her father's theater, as she was eventually awarded interscholastic medals by Oklahoma University for her musical talent and her accomplishments as a contralto singer.

By 1987, as with many historic buildings, the theater had become old and worn down. No longer in the hands of the Constantine family, it was becoming a forgotten relic, but a group led by Eileen Monger took control of the Constantine Theater and gave it a much-needed renovation. The once glorious stage was revamped into a Greek Revival style, the seating capacity was expanded to 589, and the outside edifice was restored to its former splendor. The theater now plays host to concerts, art exhibits, local variety shows, and wedding receptions. However, renovations have been known to stir up paranormal activity in old buildings.

An apparition of a woman has been seen on the premises on rare occasions, but the reporting of this goes all the way back to 1906 when the theater was still the Pawhuska House Hotel. At that time it was said that the apparition of a woman appeared on one of the outside balconies. More recently, the apparition of a woman has been seen on one of the indoor balconies, detailed enough that one could see the buttons on her dress. Whether or not these two women are one in the same is unknown, and some seem to think that the more recent female apparition may be one of Constantine's daughters, Sappho or Antigone.

Pawhuska in 1910. At the very end of the street is the Pawhuska House Hotel just before it was purchased and transformed into the Constantine Theater.

At times, random objects fly through the air here and footsteps can be heard throughout. A number of times disembodied sounds of a fist fight have resonated throughout, as if a couple of old cowboys are going at each other right in the middle of the theater. At other times, whispers have been heard and paranormal investigators have captured EVPs from this location.

One of the more common paranormal experiences at the Constantine Theater is *heard*, not witnessed: a ghostly gunshot, which still echoes throughout the place from over one hundred years ago. On Election Day in November 1908, Daniel Parker and Elmer Fraley became enraptured in an intense quarrel. Like something out of an old western movie, they met out in the street a few moments later for a duel. Fraley's shot was poor and only hit Parker in the foot, but Dan Parker's shot was true and he pierced Elmer's heart. Parker was arrested for killing Elmer Fraley, but the otherwise peaceful young man was later acquitted and continued his employment as a purchasing agent for a local lumber company.

On April 11, 1910, Dan was standing on the Main Street corner just outside of the Pawhuska Hotel when there was a tap on his shoulder. "Hello, Dan," was all he heard.

As Daniel Parker turned around, the barrel of a revolver was jabbed into his stomach and the hammer fired three times. He struggled to run, but he fell into the gutter. Three more shots ripped through him as he lay there, only spared a seventh because the revolver was out of bullets. Looming over him was the visage of M. F. Fraley, Elmer's father.

Crazed and in shock, Fraley fled from the scene and bolted straight through the Pawhuska House Hotel. He was apprehend just a few moments later and dragged to the county jail where he went into a manic rage. He later said, "I am sorry I had to kill him, but he killed my son and I shall never get over it."

Daniel Parker's aged father became so grief-stricken upon hearing the news his son had been murdered that his health rapidly deteriorated and he was suddenly in critical condition. Sympathizers of the Parker family initially wanted to escalate the feud further and have Fraley "dealt with," but their position subsided when they heard the man had lost his mind in jail.

Today, the shots fired by M. F. Fraley are still heard at the Constantine Theater. At any time of the day or night gunfire will suddenly ring out from seemingly nowhere. Facility caretakers, the paying public, and paranormal investigators have all heard the murderous shots. They serve as a reminder that although real Wild West duels did in fact happen, the participants of those duels were real people with families that cared for them very much, and the fallout was disastrous.

Chapter Fourteen
The Brady Theater and the Tulsa Race Riot

The historic Brady Theater was built in 1914 for use as a municipal auditorium and was simply titled Convention Hall during the initial forty years of its history. With an interior modeled after a barn and looking much more western than its current Art Deco style, the hall was the largest of its kind between Kansas City and Houston when it opened.

Over the years, hundreds of famous performers have passed through the Brady Theater, including Motley Crue, David Copperfield, Glen Campbell, Robin Williams, and U2. Back in the formative days of Convention Hall, it was performers like Italian tenor Enrico Caruso that graced the stage. Caruso had an extremely successful career spanning twenty-five years with tours all over the world. It was during one of these tours in 1920, after performing at Convention Hall, that he grew ill after an open carriage ride on a cold and wet day in Tulsa. He died a year later of pleurisy, and inflammation of the lining of the lungs that can lead to fluid collecting inside the chest cavity. Many say he attributed his Tulsa carriage ride to this development. It's also said that his spirit now haunts the Brady Theater in revenge.

While Caruso was dying in 1921, one of the ugliest events in Tulsa's history occurred on May 31st of that year — just outside the doors of the theater. The previous day, an African-American man named Dick Rowland was charged with assaulting Sarah Page, a white woman who operated the elevator in the Drexel Building. What really happened in the elevator remains a mystery, but one version of the story claims that Rowland tried to sexually attack Page. Another version states that she was knocked off balance when she accidentally stepped on Rowland's foot, and when he reached out to catch her the woman screamed.

The next day Rowland was arrested for sexual assault and throughout the community rumors of a lynching spread like wild fire. Incensed, seventy-five armed African-American men gathered outside the courthouse and offered protection services to Rowland, but the sheriff refused to allow it. National Guard Company B was mobilized to address the growing throng, and when a soldier tried to disarm one of the

African Americans, a shot was discharged. After that, pandemonium broke loose.

Fighting and shooting ensued... Buildings burned and telephone lines were cut. *The Associated Press* reported, "At 2 o'clock Wednesday morning two white people are known to be dead, a score wounded, some seriously, and reports are that many casualties as yet are not listed... Armed whites are marching through the streets. There is talk of an invasion by whites of the Negro district, known as 'Little Africa.' ... One Negro was shot to death on Fourth Street almost directly in front of Younkman's drug store."

The 1921 Tulsa Race Riot was in full swing. Three units of national guardsmen flooded in to try and restore order while Little Africa was razed and burned to the ground. Looting ran rampant, and at least 5,000 African Americans fled the city amidst the anguish. The total number that died in the chaos is a bit sketchy, but has been estimated at one hundred to three hundred, and it's generally believed that the number of Caucasians that died has been underestimated. Ironically, Dick Rowland was never charged for the crime it was thought he committed, but indictments stemming from the riot were brought down on five city police officers.

Race Riot detainees being marched to Convention Hall. *Courtesy of the University of Tulsa.*

The entire city was thrown into tumult, so it's unknown whether or not anyone died in the Brady Theater during the riot. However, given its close proximity to the epicenter, many believe it is likely. Some rumors claim that the auditorium was used as a morgue for riot victims. Other claims range from the theater being used as a refuge for those fleeing the scene to the building being used as a place of torture. Aside from the recent surfacing of a few photos showing African Americans being escorted to the theater, there are no hard facts to corroborate the stories.

While there are no scare-you-out-of-your-wits ghost stories told about the Brady Theater, employees and visitors alike share in their experiences there. Equipment failure is quite common at the theater. While setting up for major performances, electronics notoriously fail or give out, delaying the show. At any time of the day or night, lights reportedly turn on and off on their own and odd noises cascade down from the rafters. Some have heard the faint echo of screams emanate throughout the building. Could these be the victims of the race riot?

If you come to take in a show at the Brady Theater, you just may have an extra visitor sitting with you.

The chaos at Convention Hall, now the Brady Theater, during the Tulsa Race Riot of 1921. *Courtesy of the University of Tulsa.*

Chapter Fifteen

Gilcrease Museum and Home

Gilcrease Museum in Tulsa is home to the largest and most comprehensive collection of art and artifacts of the American West in the world. This collection was the passion of Thomas Gilcrease, who assembled more than 10,000 works of art, a library of 100,000 items, and more than 250,000 archaeological and ethnological items, and then opened the museum in 1949. Considering that spirits can attach themselves to objects, it is not surprising that the museum is also haunted.

The sound of phantom children are heard playing throughout the Gilcrease Home.
Courtesy of Cathy Nance.

Born in Robeline, Louisiana, on February 8, 1890, William Thomas Gilcrease spent much of his childhood on Creek Nation tribal lands in Indian Territory since his mother was of Creek lineage. That lineage enabled him to acquire a 160-acre parcel of land about twenty miles southwest of Tulsa when the federal government dissolved the Indian Nations land and distributed it into private ownership. Gilcrease was quite fortunate with his acquisition: in 1905 drillers struck oil in the huge Glenn Pool Reserve on which his land sat. By the time he was just twenty years of age, Thomas Gilcrease was a multi-millionaire.

He nurtured his business at first, and by 1917 he had thirty-two oil wells on his land. In 1922, he formed the Gilcrease Oil Company and soon discovered a new oil-producing stratum near Wetumka. The company expanded into Kansas and Texas, and he gained controlling interest in several banks throughout the region. However, after extensive travel to Europe that included tours of many libraries and museums, Gilcrease developed a passion to assemble his own American collection of artifacts.

He began collecting as early as 1922, but he amassed most of the content after 1939. At the time there were very few who were interested in collecting Native American art or artifacts of the Old West, and Thomas was more than happy to take the material off their hands. He had a personal philosophy that, "every man must leave a track and it might as well be a good one," so in 1949 he constructed a building to house the thousands of pieces of material he had gathered. Even after opening the museum he continued collecting more art, old documents, books, and artifacts to add to the collection. In 1955, he deeded his collection to the City of Tulsa, prior to his passing in 1962, but he hasn't necessarily departed from his massive assemblage.

Gilcrease's favorite location to visit on the grounds was the beautifully manicured gardens, and he is often seen there still to this day walking amongst the foliage. There's a high rate of turnover of security guards at the museum, and much of this has been attributed to seeing the apparition of the museum's founder. Thomas has also been seen at his former house, which holds Art Education classes put on by the museum's Education Department. The curators of the home describe his demeanor as friendly, and he has appeared to them as if he was saying, "Hello."

An interesting haunt of the Gilcrease House is that of the sound of children playing throughout the home. During a short period of time in the 1940s, the house was used as an orphanage for Indian children, beginning in 1943 until Thomas moved back into the home in 1949 after a stint in San Antonio. It is not know whether any of the children died in the home, but there were a number of diseases and epidemics across the area at the time and it's possible that one or more of the children suffered from one. The child ghosts have also been known to play out in the garden area like Thomas Gilcrease.

Various paranormal investigative teams have been to the museum, house, and grounds and have collected some interesting evidence. EVPs of a woman singing and men arguing have been recorded. Strange temperature fluctuations have been noted and technical malfunctions of electronic equipment have occurred. Some of their items would go missing only to appear later in odd places.

Perhaps there's a bit of a prankster in Thomas Gilcrease, or perhaps it's one of the Native American children playing a game. In either case, when one comes to explore the museum and grounds, he or she may be taking a tour beside the person who put the whole collection together.

Chapter Sixteen

Belvidere Mansion

Is it a house or is it a castle? That's a common question one asks themselves when first gazing upon the Belvidere Mansion and its distinguished turrets located in Claremore. It's an enormous Gothic structure that was built during the early 1900s when Mr. John M. Bayless of the Cassville and Western Railroad arrived from Cassville, Missouri, with his family.

The mansion is Victorian in architecture and made of brick with a tile roof and a tower on each of the four corners of the structure. Just the third story ballroom itself is 3,000 square feet and is adorned with gold chandeliers and sconces. The ceilings are vaulted and feature an old-fashioned skylight, and the windows are covered in lace.

While construction on the house began in 1902, Bayless helped to establish business in Claremore. He built the three-story Windsor Opera House, an athletic building with an indoor swimming pool, and the Sequoyah Hotel, which housed some pretty interesting people in 1913. George Washington Eaton, one of the founding fathers of Claremore, had discovered hydrogen sulfide and sulfur water and began marketing it as "radium water" — water that was supposed to help heal rheumatism, stomach problems, and eczema. Princess Stephania Kaunitz traveled all the way from Vienna, Austria, to try the water for herself in March 1913, and was happy to discover baseball's Pittsburgh Pirates were also staying at the Sequoyah Hotel. She made it known that she wanted to meet future Hall of Famer Honus Wagner, "The Flying Dutchman." The Sequoyah no longer stands, and neither do any of the other Bayless constructions, save the Belvidere Mansion.

Unfortunately, Bayless never saw the completion of his family's home. On June 2, 1907, John M. Bayless was rushed to the hospital with severe stomach pains. He died that night on the operating table of appendicitis, just six months before the completion of Belvidere Mansion. It was with heavy hearts that Mrs. Mary Bayless and her children moved into the large, castle-like house to begin their lives together without John.

Six years later, the family sustained tragedy again. Daughter Bland had married William Farris Martin and moved to Kansas City, but something went terribly wrong on September 11, 1913. Bland was found strung from a curtain rod in a doorway, killing herself after complaining of a pain in the back of her neck. William's mother had seen Bland that day and remarked about the neck pain, "I thought nothing of it at the time but now I believe she must have suffered some sort of temporary derangement. She and my son were happily married and were building a new home in Morningside Park. I know of no cause for her to take her own life."

Is it a house or a castle? Belvidere in 1910.

By 1928 all the Bayless children had moved out of the extravagant mansion, and their mother, Mary, passed away. None of the children moved into the home, which remained vacant for a few years until it was finally sold in the 1930s. For the next thirty years it was used as an apartment building. The classic structure was becoming old and worn down, so the Rogers County Historical Society stepped in and purchased the Belvidere Mansion. They've been operating it ever since.

Over the years, stories of both John Bayless and his daughter, Bland, haunting the mansion have surfaced. One day there was a woman who came to the mansion for a tour and encountered a man on the front porch. He was quite cordial with her and told her he was happy with the way the house looked and was being maintained. The comment seemed a little unusual, so when she entered she asked the staff about the man. Baffled about who may be outside, they went out to talk to him, but the man was gone. During her tour, the woman was shown a picture of John M. Bayless and she exclaimed that he had been the man she saw on the porch.

At other times, a woman's voice can be heard throughout the mansion whispering to visitors. A man taking a tour one afternoon entered Bland's room and heard a woman ask him, "Who are you?" He searched around for the source of the question, but not a soul was in the room. On one particular occasion, one of the curators of the mansion saw her grandson talking to a woman that fit Bland's description. Others have felt the heavy weight of sadness and then the burn of a rope on their neck. After her suicide, did Bland return home to Claremore to try and recapture the days of her youth?

Other incidents at the mansion have been reported, such as strange lights flickering in the upstairs windows, shadow masses being spotted throughout the home, and toilets flushing on their own. However, most of the stories always come back to John and Bland, both early to depart this life and yet the two that remain lingering on at Belvidere Mansion.

Chapter Seventeen

Labadie Mansion Legends

The remnants of this once great home near Copan could be called "The Home of Legends" for all the tales associated with it. Perhaps the eeriness of the remaining stone walls, crumbling year by year, spurn a bit of creativity in passing storytellers, but a number of different words have been spoken about the old Labadie mansion, whether it be by campfire, paper, or blog. What really happened there and which of these tales contain pieces of the truth?

One tale describes the sad story of Frank and Samantha Labadie, a married couple who could not conceive a child. They owned a loyal black slave named Enos Parsons who had refused freedom even though slavery had been abolished. In the winter of 1892, Samantha had an affair with Enos and conceived a child. Her husband, Frank, was delighted at first not knowing he wasn't the father, but upon seeing the race of the child when the baby was born he went mad. Frank shot Parsons with a .44 Henry rifle and dumped his body in a nearby creek. Some claimed that instead of floating downstream, the body sank and the remains are still there to this day.

Many years later in 1935, Frank started becoming unsettled and claimed the ghost of Enos Parsons was haunting him. On April 1st of that year, he could no longer handle the hauntings, so he took out his pistol and killed both Samantha and himself. Their spirits are said to still roam the old home. Frank is known to get aggressive with trespassers and pushes them as they walk through. Some say the woods around the creek are haunted by Enos Parsons, carrying the rifle that killed him.

In 1980, the legend of "The April Fools' Ghost" began with a story that was submitted to *Green Country Living*. According to the piece, three teenage boys had heard that Mr. Labadie had gone insane on April Fools' Day and killed his family by throwing them out of the third story attic window. He then killed himself as well. Upon hearing that the ruins were the site of a tragic murder, the three boys set out to find the old house and uncover its secrets. The dramatized story stirred up controversy with the descendants of the Labadie family.

Riled up over the assertion that their uncle had been accused of a murder-suicide, Blanche Labadie Mounts and Winifred V. Labadie wrote the editor of *Green Country Living* to clear up the matter. They explained that on April 1, 1935, Frank and Samantha Labadie were found dead in their home of carbon monoxide asphyxiation. The house was poorly ventilated and the fumes from a gas-burning stove overwhelmed them. The residence that they lived in was not even the ruined house that the curious seek, although it's in the vicinity. Burned twice by fire, the stone ruins was a house owned by their son, George, one of four children the couple had together.

What is the real story, and if the Labadie's quietly lived their life near Copan, then how does Enos Parsons fit in the tale? Interestingly enough, the Labadie Cemetery has a grave plot for Enos Parsons, but it's marked with the ominous notation, "Believed to be buried here." Is his body really buried there, or is it resting at the bottom of a creek?

Ghost seekers trudge up the hill to the ruins, hoping to catch a glimpse of the spirits from days gone by. Many who venture up have experienced malfunctions with their flashlights and electronic equipment. Strange smells and aromas waft up from the remains of the old house while the names of those that visit emanate from the darkness. Apparitions have been sighted staring out from the second floor window where there is no floor, and on occasion, when one turns to leave from investigating the area, ghostly flames alight in the ruined fireplace with little tongues of fire licking the still air.

The type of rifle that may have killed Enos Parsons... according to one story.

Part 4

Southeast Oklahoma

Chapter Eighteen

Fort Washita and Aunt Jane

In 1803, Thomas Jefferson wrote future president of Tippecanoe fame, William Henry Harrison, "To promote this disposition to exchange lands, which they have to spare and we want, for necessaries, which we have to spare and they want, we shall push our trading uses, and be glad to see the good and influential individuals among them run in debt, because we observe that when these debts get beyond what the individuals can pay, they become willing to lop them off by a cession of lands.... In this way our settlements will gradually circumscribe and approach the Indians, and they will in time either incorporate with us as citizens of the United States, or remove beyond the Mississippi."

Although this idea of transplanting Native Americans out of the east took some time to manifest, the Cherokee finally ceded large tracts of their land in Georgia for land in Arkansas in 1817. The perceived success of this move led to President Andrew Jackson signing in to law the Indian Removal Act in 1830, which forced the "Five Civilized Tribes" out of the east and into what is now Oklahoma (then called Indian Territory). These tribes consisted of the Cherokee, Chickasaw, Choctaw, Creek, and Seminole, but their presence in the new land did not please the pre-existing Plains Indians. In the southeastern portion of Indian Territory, Fort Washita was built to help protect the Chickasaw and Choctaw who were trying to establish their community.

Established in 1842 by General Zachary Taylor, permanent buildings began being constructed in 1843 and grew over the years to include a barracks, hospital, surgeon's quarters, library, bar, newspaper, and even a bowling alley. When pioneers rushed out west to California for gold in the 1850s, Fort Washita served as a busy refuge and supply point. The fort temporarily closed, however, in 1858, but was soon reopened when aggressive Comanche activity in the area picked up. It was abandoned again in 1861 by Union troops during the Civil War after Fort Sumter in South Carolina was captured, but it was quickly seized by the Confederacy.

Valuing the facility more than the Union, the Confederacy transformed Fort Washita into a regional headquarters, major supply depot, and medical center for Confederate troops. After fighting the Battle of Honey Springs, the largest Civil War battle in Indian Territory, General Douglas Cooper briefly commanded the fort and is now buried there in an unmarked and unknown grave. When the war ended, the Confederate troops decided they'd be damned if the Union controlled the fort again and set it ablaze as they marched out in August 1865.

The old barracks where soldiers and the Colbert family lived. Does the spirit of Aunt Jane now reside here?

With nothing but disintegrating stone walls and a few scattered buildings remaining, the Department of the Interior assumed control of Fort Washita in 1870. They deemed the old fort obsolete and deeded the property to Charley and Abbie Davis Colbert, Chickasaw Indians, who rebuilt the barracks for their family to use as a home. According to the legend, in the morning following their first night in the house, the Colbert's discovered their thirty-two dogs were missing. Charley was able to track them all down, but the next night they disappeared again. This went on for several days, spooking the family, but it suddenly stopped. Charley went on to hold the high office of Auditor, Chickasaw Nation, and became recognized as one if its most distinguished men.

The fort remained in the hands of the Chickasaw Nation until 1962 when the State of Oklahoma purchased it and placed Fort Washita in control of the Oklahoma Historical Society. The site has been restored and is now listed in the National Register of Historic Places.

The mysterious legend of Aunt Jane, the name on one of the headstones at the site, has haunted Fort Washita for over a century. There are three different tales to her demise, but they all contain one constant — she was decapitated. This consistency exists because the apparition of Aunt Jane around the fort is seen as a woman in a mid 1800s dress wandering the ruins in search of her missing head.

In the first tale, Aunt Jane was a free Negro working for the Union during the Civil War and went to Fort Washita to spy on the Confederate troops stationed there. She was a poor spy, however, and when she was discovered by the Confederacy she was put to death by beheading. Her head and her body were then buried separately.

In the second tale, Aunt Jane is actually the white wife of an officer stationed at the fort. Rumor floated around that she always liked to carry $20 in gold with her, and one day when she was outside the confines of the fort she was ambushed by thieves. They stole her money and in the struggle one of the thieves cut off her head.

Finally, the third story pits Jane in the middle of a lover's quarrel. Again, she was the wife of an officer at Fort Washita, and on the night of her death her husband was out on patrol. When he came home that dark night he found Jane in bed with another soldier. In a violent rage, he charged the lovers and decapitated them, then afterward tossed their heads into the river.

A number of other eerie incidents have happened at the fort as well. A number of dark masses and shadows have been seen moving all about the area while mists have risen up near the old Confederate cemetery. If the shadows and mists aren't enough, colored light anomalies dance along the road nearby. Voices have been heard amongst the ruins, with disembodied footsteps and galloping horse hooves intermingled at times. Apparitions of Civil War soldiers fade in and out, sometimes as a single entity and other times as a group.

In the mid-1990s, a living history group spent a few nights at Fort Washita in the Bohanan Cabin. This cabin was originally built in Durant between 1865 and 1870, but had been moved to the fort property for the living history demonstrations. The first night, one woman woke up to the startling sensation of being strangled. After things settled down and the ladies tried to go back to sleep, another woman felt a strong presence hovering over her. The following night they all had dreams of suffocation. There was also a strange incident in which one of the historic corsets they brought along had all of its strings mysteriously disappear.

The Bohanan Cabin... People have felt like they were being strangled by an unseen force here.

On September 26, 2010, the Fort Washita barracks was mysteriously set ablaze with total damages nearing $2 million.

Chapter Nineteen

The Ritz Theater

The Ritz Theater building was originally built as a two-business establishment in Shawnee on land purchased from the railroad in 1896. Shawnee was first settled after the Civil War by Indian tribes that had been uprooted to the area by the federal government, and later by cattle drivers and Quaker missionaries in the 1870s. During the September 22, 1891, land run, John Beard, Etta B. Ray, Elijah Alley, and James Farral staked their claims on the land that now make up the town of Shawnee. Beard and Etta Ray got married and their first homestead, Beard Cabin, still stands in the town. The Beard's were insistent on the railroad coming through Shawnee instead of Tecumseh, so they sold off 250 acres of land to the Choctaw, Oklahoma and Gulf Railroad in 1894. It was a parcel of this land that Wesley G. Montgomery and his wife, Dora, bought in 1896.

Montgomery first operated half of the building as a furniture store, and his father-in-law, William Blackman, bought the other half and opened a small grocery store. Historic maps show that the functions of these two sides seemed to change over the next few years with Montgomery's side as a dry goods and grocery store and Williams side as a drug store in 1901. By 1904, Montgomery's establishment was a grocery store only, and in 1906 the first official name for the building was established as Wallace Mann Drug Store. It's believed that by then Williams had rented out his side to capitalist William Blackman. By 1909, Montgomery began renting the upstairs rooms as The Gordon Hotel. It was a lot of action in a short period of time.

This back-and-forth operation finally settled down in 1911 after Thomas Ellis bought out Montgomery's side and transformed it into the Cozy Theater for "moving pictures." Montgomery continued to manage the Cozy and lived upstairs in the renamed Savoy Hotel after he and Dora divorced in 1913. Ownership continued to change hands, including a short stint under the ownership of Leo Montgomery, Wesley's son, but it finally settled upon Jake Jones in 1916. Known for opening Shawnee's first confectioneries and ice cream stores, Jones ran the building as the Cozy Hotel and Boarding House. Leo stayed on as the theater's projectionist, and Wesley continued to board at the hotel until his death in the early 1920s, although he was no longer in management.

The Cozy underwent extensive remodeling in 1924. A brand new lobby was added, some of the best seats of the day were brought in to replace the old ones, and a new pipe organ was installed to play along during silent films. Two years after the renovations the name was changed to "The Ritz," and in 1927 the theater became the first in Shawnee to begin showing talking motion pictures.

Those that work at the Ritz Theater still linger there into the afterlife.

The Jones family continued to operate the theater for decades. In 1945 the boarding house portion of the building closed, but the theater continued to be updated and was the first to utilize Dolby stereo in Oklahoma. In 1988, however, the Ritz Theater made its last run as a motion picture house with *Willow*. Twelve years later, the Jones family gave the theater to the Society for Revitalization of Downtown Shawnee (SRDS), and the theater holds four to six performances per year, covering such classics as *The Nutcracker Suite* and the works of Shakespeare.

The most legendary ghost at The Ritz is believed to be the spirit of Leo Montgomery. Leo first began working as the theater projectionist for his father in 1913, and only intended to work there for another year after Jake Jones bought the establishment in 1916. However, the lovely Viola Cora Cates who worked across the street at what was then the Palace of Sweets Candy shop caught his eye. They married in 1926 and Leo spent another fifty-two years working at the Ritz. They also lived for a time in the boarding house above the theater.

Leo had quite a system set up in the projection booth. He strategically placed a mirror in the room to view the film's progress from an easy chair he kept there, and was warned when to change the reel via a bell system he'd devised. He wouldn't watch the films, but would listen to the radio or write short rhymes, which earned him the nickname of "Postcard Philosopher." The *Shawnee News-Star* quoted him in 1948, "For me to go to the show would be just like a lifeguard going for a swim on his day off."

One day, a movie had concluded, but the reel kept spinning without Leo having stopped it. Perplexed, another one of the workers at the theater went to check on the problem and discovered that Leo had passed away in the projection room. An autopsy later revealed that the 83-year-old had suffered a heart attack. Leo Street in Shawnee is named in his memory.

Locals insist that Leo Montgomery never left Ritz Theater and his spirit still roams there today. People hear him walking up to the projector room and there are random times in which the projector starts rolling or the lights turn on. There's also been at least one sighting of Leo Montgomery described as "an older white gentleman wearing a vest and pants pulled up kind of high" as well as "balding."

Charlotte Patterson of the Ritz Revitalization Society stated in a 2008 interview, "I've been in and out of this building all hours of the day and night for ten years now. We would notice things not being quite the same way, and there are only three people that have keys to the building."

Paranormal investigations of the theater have revealed similar experiences of misplaced objects in the boarding house area. OKPRI's official report from their website states:

> "On our initial visit there was a Bible that just appeared in the middle of one of the rooms so one of our investigators marked the Bible by placing it on a sheet of paper and then marking around the paper. Since we had investigated the Ritz Theater numerous times, we had set up little experiments throughout it and strangely enough the Bible stayed in place for months before finally moving again. Our investigators took pictures and documented the placement of the Bible both times that it moved. A bank book was also found and was in pristine condition to be lying in the middle of the hallway floor."

Some believe that the spirit of a young woman named Amelia who caught pneumonia and died at the age of nineteen is one who haunts the boarding house. An Italian man and an older woman in dated clothing are also said to roam the upstairs rooms, but it appears that the ghost of Leo Montgomery is the most prevalent, checking in on the theater in which he spent most of his life.

Chapter Twenty

The Eskridge Hotel

The town of Wynnewood was established in 1886, but was originally called Walner after its founder, John Walner, a resident of the Chickasaw Nation. When the railroad came through in 1887 it was renamed to Wynnewood after the Pennsylvania home town of one of the railroad officials. The connection helped the town establish a solid base to trade its rich agriculture of pecans, peaches, corn, wheat, oats, alfalfa, and cotton. The residents of Wynnewood soon built around it a cottonseed oil company, four cotton gins, and a lumberyard, as well as a variety of shops that created a bustling town.

During the early 1900s, Pinckney Reid Eskridge, a "drummer" or cotton wholesaler, traveled along the Santa Fe Railroad from Texas to Kansas working his business, and found many of the hotel beds rather lumpy and uncomfortable. When he discovered that other traveling salesmen had the same complaint, he decided to build his own hotel that provided comforts to travelers the right way. Wynnewood appeared to be the most thriving town on his sales route, so he established his hotel there in 1907, the year of Oklahoma's statehood. The three-story brick building with pure cotton Ostermoor mattresses helped Wynnewood become dubbed "Queen City of the Famous Washita Valley."

In a bizarre incident within its first year of operation, blood was spilled in the hotel's barbershop. Chief of Police Charles Litchfield and his deputy, John Witt, arrived at the shop on April 13, 1908, to arrest the proprietor John Norman for breaking the Sunday closing law. However, one of the customers in the barbershop at the time, Bob Jarrett, who had a history with Litchfield and didn't like the man, decided to interfere. According to the local paper, when told to back off, Jarrett "pulled a knife and started to carve the chief of police. The deputy got excited and instead of grappling with Jarrett, grasped Litchfield and held him while Jarrett cut the officer." Litchfield survived, but would no longer serve as police chief.

Two years later, Charles Litchfield was a restaurant proprietor in Wynnewood and found himself on the other side of the law. At the hotel on the morning of July 19, 1910, Litchfield's sixteen-year-old daughter, Willie, met with one of her father's best friends, Will Collins, and they agreed to meet up later that afternoon and go out for an automobile ride. They were lovers, though they were both separately married, and Willie had just recently conceived Will's child. Willie had developed a bad reputation around town, and other friends of Will's had warned him to stay away from the girl.

"Will, I wouldn't go out with this girl," R. T. Norman cautioned.

Collins responded, "The girl is going wrong, and there will be a killing over it, and I never intend to go out with her again." However, he did continue to go out with Willie and even told her that he was going to get rid of his wife.

Clif Cunningham warned Collins of another aspect of the situation. "If I was you, I would stop that. I wouldn't go any further with that. Litchfield is a man that will kill you if he catches you."

Collins laughed. "Well, when it comes to that Old Betsy makes me equal to any of them," and he patted his shirt where a gun was stowed.

The 1912 court record of Willie's testimony at her father's hearing tells her version of what happened that July 19 after her meeting with Will Collins at the hotel:

"After getting into the automobile, deceased took a bottle of whisky and a six-shooter out of his pockets, and placed them behind him. That, at the request of deceased, witness took a drink of whisky. That at this time witness was perfectly sober. That they drove the automobile out to the lake... and they got out of the car. ... At this time witness had begun to feel the effects of the whisky she had been drinking, and asked for some water. ... Deceased then placed his arms around witness, and kissed her, and lifted her off of the ground, and said he loved her, and they both drank beer together. That after they were through drinking the beer deceased proposed intercourse with witness, to which witness did not give a definite answer. That witness and deceased then scuffled around, and he pushed her back against a tree. That just then appellant came up. That before this deceased had laid his gun about three feet from them on the ground. That she was pushed to the ground and had raised up, and, as she raised up, the deceased pushed her to one side. That just as this was done she saw the smoke from the pistol in her father's hands. That witness at this time was so excited and intoxicated she does not remember hearing the shot of the pistol."

Charles Litchfield testified that when he appeared on the scene he didn't at first see his daughter, but heard her pleading and crying. When he ran up to her, Collins tossed Willie aside and made a move for his six-shooter, which had been lying on the ground just a few feet away. Collins was able to grab it, but Litchfield fired off two rounds from his own gun. He told the court, "I just lost all presence of mind. I found him trying to have intercourse with my daughter, and by the time I saw the condition of things as it was, why he was in a position to get hold of arms, and so it all happened about the same time. I come up on Mr. Collins, and he was trying to have sexual intercourse with my girl, with my daughter, and had her backed up against a tree."

Charles was originally convicted of murder, but on September 21, 1912, the court of criminal appeals upheld his right to prevent the dishonor of his daughter. In order to justify the homicide, the court quoted an ancient Jewish law that condones a murder to prevent the commission of a felony. Charles Litchfield was a free man and soon after he, his wife, and his younger children moved to Texas.

The historic Eskridge Hotel where some guests haven't yet checked out.

The Eskridge Hotel hasn't changed much over the years since those days. The tin ceiling is still in place, the original guest keys hang near the desk, and many artifacts from the early 1900s are on display in a museum that has been in operation of the hotel since 1973. The exhibits are designed to depict early Oklahoman life while still retaining the charm of the Eskridge. These include a doctor's office, dress shop, and a tool and tack room. Throughout each one, dark shadows and footsteps of the past are commonly seen and heard.

The "Dress Room," which contains an assortment of period dresses displayed on mannequins, has activity that has been repeatedly reported by a variety of witnesses. The mannequins take on a life of their own and are moved about the room. Furniture and other objects in the room are moved around as well while ballroom music is heard coming from down the hall. Is one of the ladies from yesteryear busy shopping?

In many rooms throughout the old hotel rapping and knocking noises are heard. People feel like they're being followed or watched, and sometimes they are even touched by something unseen. Disembodied voices emanate over the air waves on the second and third floors.

While there are no stories specifically associated with the haunting of someone that worked at, owned, or stayed at the hotel, there are some indications that the spirits there may be transient, en route from other locations. Perhaps they find the Eskridge a safe haven because it's retained in an early twentieth century state. One such spirit goes by the name of "Elizabeth" who lingers in the hallway but stays out of the rooms where other spirits stay. Another is a man in Room #28 who enjoys having a cloth put on the table in the room and seemingly likes oranges since the smell of orange has been known to waft from this room.

The haunts are colorful and varied at the historic building. You never know who or what you may encounter at the Eskridge Hotel, but it's a wonderful look into the days gone by.

Chapter Twenty-One

Sense of Charm

Over the past one hundred years the Sense of Charm shop in downtown Shawnee has seen its share of faces, both inside and outside. It has sold dry goods, shoes, dresses, art, organic foods, toys, and gifts through numerous tenants and a variety of different names. It debuted as The Aurora Store, a dry goods shop run by Max Herskowitz, a Hungarian immigrant who had moved to Oklahoma with his wife and eleven children after brief stays in New York and Ohio. Max passed away in 1911, but the family continued to own the property and lease out the shop until 1945, the store front serving as three different dry goods shops and two different shoe stores.

Felice Gold of California bought the property from the Herskowitz Estate, and for the next twenty-five years it served as Arden's Dress Shop. It was a staple of downtown Shawnee and the longest tenured store to serve at the location, but Arden's eventually was sold off as well, and over the past forty years the shop has had nine different tenants mingled with a brief period of vacancy that encompassed 1992.

There may be a couple different spirits lingering around the old shop, but the predominant one appears to be that of a young boy. The owners have heard the running footsteps of a small child in the balloon room when no one else is there, and some of the paranormal antics include knocking dolls off of shelves and the whisper of a boy's voice. Witnesses have said they believe the boy is saying he's thirsty, and a captured audio EVP picked up on him calling for a kitten. A faint apparition of the boy has also once been seen.

It's also believed the presence of a man is there, but it's hard to determine which spirit is creating some of the activity. Lights and electronic equipment get turned on, doors slam shut, and loud bangs as if something has fallen emanate throughout the shop when nothing has actually taken a spill. There have been a few times when some of these bangs are from objects that have randomly dropped to the floor, and those incidents include a large cabinet and wooden figurines. The causes of these strange accidents are unknown.

It hasn't been determined who these spirits are and from which era they may have come, but they do make the present-day Sense of Charm shop quite lively.

The quaint Sense of Charm with its mischievous spirits.

Part 5

Northwest Oklahoma

Chapter Twenty-Two

The Second Life of John Wilkes Booth

I can't seem to get away from this man. When I wrote *Ghosts of Maryland*, two of my prominent ghost stories featured the escape of John Wilkes Booth after his assassination of President Abraham Lincoln. Considering the tragic history behind the event, plus the hauntings of the Surratt House and the Samuel Mudd House (*especially* the Samuel Mudd House), it made sense for me to cover that as well. When I came out to Oklahoma and heard that there was a claim of Booth's death in the state, I was both baffled and intrigued. The following is an account of this fantastic legend.

Accomplished actor and Confederate sympathizer, John Wilkes Booth, was tracked down to a barn near Port Royal, Virginia, after having fled from Ford's Theater and remarkably trekking through Maryland and across the Potomac River with a broken leg. He refused to surrender and the barn was set ablaze. Traditional history tells us that Booth was gunned down by Sgt. Boston Corbett through the barn walls minutes later when he still hadn't emerged. However, there is a conspiracy theory that suggests otherwise.

A faction of people, including some of John Wilkes Booth's descendants, believe Booth escaped Virginia and the man that was killed at the barn was someone else, possibly James William Boyd, a man who somewhat resembled Booth but had red hair. Did the man who was shot have red hair? Identification of the body at the scene was made by Sgt. Corbett who fired at the black silhouette inside the barn against orders. There were also a few oddities about the autopsy.

Following the death at the barn, there was a delay in moving the body to Alexandria on a tugboat that would later deliver Booth to the ironclad *Montauk*, which was being repaired at the Washington Navy Yard. Since the body's condition was rapidly deteriorating, an autopsy was ordered to be performed as soon as possible by Surgeon General Joseph K. Barnes. Witnesses were quickly gathered for identification of the corpse. William Crowninshield, the Montauk's acting master stated he recognized Booth's general appearance, but there was no solid evidence that the two had ever really known each other. Charles Dawson, a hotel clerk, said he'd known Booth from the initials tattooed on his wrist, but he identified the wrong wrist. Dr. Frederick May who had removed a tumor from Booth's neck at first stated that there was no resemblance in the corpse to Booth, but later amended his statement to claim that the scar on the neck was similar to Booth's. Nobody that was actually personally close to Booth was brought in for this autopsy.

Years later in the spring of 1872, lawyer Finis L. Bates met John St. Helen when St. Helen was supposed to be a witness for the defendant in a case in which a man was being accused of selling tobacco and whiskey without a license out of a storehouse in Glenrose Mills, Texas. St. Helen, however, did not want to appear before the Federal Court. The reason was not because he was actually the guilty party in the case and not the accused. Breathing hard and his body under distress, St. Helen began telling Bates, "Now, that I have employed you and paid your retainer fee, you, as my lawyer, will and must keep secret such matters as I shall confide in you touching my legal interest and personal safety."

The lawyer assured him and St. Helen continued, "I say to you, as my attorney, that my true name is not John St. Helen, as you know me and suppose me to be, and for this reason I cannot afford to go to Tyler before Federal Court, in fear that my true identity be discovered. … I ask that you take your client, indicted in the Federal Court at Tyler, and get him clear of this charge, of which he is certainly not guilty, using your best judgment in his behalf and for my protection. For this service I will pay your fee and all costs incident to the trial and trip."

Finis Bates agreed to the terms and went to the Federal Court at Tyler without John St. Helen as a witness. An agreement was reached with the court, and the defendant paid a fine for the transgression, but used the money from St. Helen to pay it. Bates and St. Helen had a few more interactions in Glenrose Mills, Bates interested in the man's eloquence and ability to entertain those around him. By July, however, John St. Helen had moved twenty miles northeast, to Granbury.

There are records of a man by the name of John St. Helen performing regularly at the Granbury Opera House in the Texas town during the 1870s. Like Booth, he was an accomplished Shakespearian actor. Other physical characteristics were identical between the two, such as the deformed right thumb, the mismatched eyebrows, and St. Helen walked with a limp from an old severe leg injury. It's also said that this John St. Helen, who tended bar as his main profession in Granbury, would drink himself into a stupor every April 14, the anniversary of the Lincoln assassination, yet remained sober every other day. Finis

Bates also claimed that St. Helen would periodically return to Glenrose Mills, and when he did he would entertain Bates in his office with performances of Shakespeare. The opposite was also true when Bates would travel to Granbury.

In 1877, John St. Helen took ill and he feared he was on his deathbed. Even his physician thought the man was going to die. It was there at Granbury late one night that John St. Helen claimed he was actually John Wilkes Booth. He revealed to those to whom he confessed where they could find the Lincoln murder weapon wrapped in a newspaper clipping about the president's death. However, instead of passing away, St. Helen's condition improved. Shortly after regaining health, he fled the area.

The notorious John Wilkes Booth prior to assassinating President Abraham Lincoln. *Courtesy of Duke University Libraries.*

A few years later there was a teacher and thespian who had arrived in Bandera, Texas, and was similar in description to John Wilkes Booth and John St. Helen. He walked with a limp, spoke with a southern accent, and within three years had fallen in love with the daughter of a local cattle magnate. She accepted his proposal of marriage and a date was set. One of the bride's family members had been an investigator on the Booth case, and hadn't been convinced that Booth was truly dead. The investigator questioned the groom-to-be for a short time, during which the southerner suddenly stated that he was growing a bit ill and went to lie down. In the dead of the night, the teacher from Bandera disappeared into the Texas landscape.

Decades passed until the tale picked up again in 1903. A man named David E. George, a poor painter of houses by profession, was living at the boarding house at the Grand Avenue Hotel in Enid, Oklahoma. Locals claimed he sometimes said, "I killed the best man that ever lived." Depressed, George administered poison to himself in the lonely hotel room and for the following few hours screamed in agony as the fatal dose snaked its way into his system. The screams roused the boarding house staff and they rushed into the room to discover what was wrong. George told them what he had done and also gave a deathbed confession that he was really John Wilkes Booth. It was also revealed later that he had given this same confession to Mrs. C. A. Harper, a local preacher's wife, when he grew ill one day a couple years prior. However, he frightened her with threats after he recovered. Found upon his body after he died was a letter addressed to Finis Bates, who was then living in Memphis, Tennessee.

The following day, David George was embalmed and put on display at Kaufman's Funeral Parlor so that someone from the public could claim him. The locals remarked about his resemblance to John Wilkes Booth and the doctor who confirmed his death also noted that George had once suffered from a severe broken leg. As the throng of people increased to get a glimpse of this man, crowd leaders grew up that enticed the lot to demand the body be handed over to a lynch mob. Police were brought in to maintain order, and word spread about the rising discontent. Junius B. Booth, nephew of John Wilkes, went to Enid and identified the body as his uncle, but he did not claim it.

Upon hearing about the death and description of the man in Enid, Oklahoma, Finis L. Bates traveled to the town and examined the corpse. Bates claimed that the body was that of the man that he had once known as John St. Helen, and David George was released to him upon payment of the embalming fee. However, the tale doesn't stop there.

Bates may have befriended John St. Helen, but there was no rest, no funeral, nor any burial for the body of David E. George. In 1904, the mummified corpse of the man that resembled and claimed to be John Wilkes Booth was put on display at the St. Louis World's Fair. Bates began writing a book about an alternate history of the man who had shot and killed Abraham Lincoln, and he leased out the body to a number of carnivals that put it on display as a sideshow.

Bates's book, *The Escape and Suicide of John Wilkes Booth*, was published in 1908, and a number of suitors emerged desiring to purchase the mummy of David George. Henry Ford was actually one who expressed some interest, but whether it was to avoid public scrutiny or he truly started disbelieving the Booth legend from Enid, he withdrew. Bates eventually sold the corpse to a traveling circus where it remained a sideshow until disappearing to time. Its last appearance was in the mid-1970s and is now believed to be tucked away in a storehouse somewhere, although that is pure speculation.

Today, both the Granbury Opera House and the old Grand Avenue Hotel, now Garfield Furniture in Enid, have reported incidents of paranormal activity. During a recent investigation by the television show, *Ghost Lab*, they believed that they captured an EVP in the ambient noise at Granbury of an entity saying, "Yes, I am John Wilkes Booth."

The room in which David E. George died at Garfield Furniture has been preserved from the day George committed suicide. Within are the same bed, chair, and wallpaper from that fateful day. All that is missing is the door to the room, which is important to note since one of the strange noises the proprietor hears at the old boarding house is that of a door slamming. Those working at the furniture store have felt like someone was looking over their shoulder when nobody was around, and the motion detectors in the basement have been set off without provocation.

There are so many mysteries associated with this tale. The obvious one is did John Wilkes Booth escape and make a life for him in the American Wild West? Were either or both John St. Helen or David E. George really John Wilkes Booth? What happened to the mummified body of David George? Can the same spirit haunt two locations at the same time? If John Wilkes Booth really did escape, then who is it that was killed by Sgt. Boston Corbett at Port Royal, Virginia?

Perhaps that answer went to the grave with the eccentric Corbett, a man who had actually castrated himself for having impure sexual thoughts. The final mystery: is it merely an interesting coincidence that the grave of Sgt. James "Boston" Corbett is located in Enid, Oklahoma?

Chapter Twenty-Three

The Knox Building

The Knox Building, home of the Enid Symphony Orchestra in downtown Enid's historic district, is a former Masonic Temple built by the Enid Masons, Lodge #80 in 1924. The Temple comprised the top two floors while the bottom three served as office space whose rent went to fund the Temple. When the Great Depression hit in the 1930s, the Masons were compelled to sell the building. Charles Knox owned a refinery in Covington as well as other property in the area and bought the structure on West Broadway, which he named after himself. A decade later, Knox steeply raised the rent at the building, and the Masons moved on. Perhaps this wasn't the wisest business decision by Mr. Knox since the building proceeded to remain vacant for the next forty years.

In the 1990s, Doug Newell, Music Director of the Enid Symphony Orchestra, bought the old Temple on the top two floors, and in 1997 spent $3.2 million renovating it into a beautiful Eighteenth Century French symphony hall that seats 340. Along with the elegant symphony hall, the facility contains the Jane Champlin Art Gallery, the Ballroom Theatre, and the Eleanor Hoehn Hornbaker Banquet Hall. Garfield County Masonic Lodge #501 also meets at the building.

The Knox Building's resident ghost is known as George. One day, Mr. Newell heard someone coming down the stairs and went to see who it was. Upon reaching the stairs, Mr. Newell encountered a short elevator repairman in a monogrammed blue work suit with a cigar in his mouth. Newell greeted the man, whose name on the suit read "George," but George didn't respond and continued to walk down the stairs. Oddly, the sound of his footsteps on the stairs ceased as he proceeded down. Mr. Newell decided to call the elevator repair company and thank them for sending out George, but the company told him that he must be mistaken because they hadn't sent anyone out to the Knox Building.

As Newell stayed longer in Enid, the more he began hearing about the local ghost stories, including ones which involved the Symphony center. He was surprised to discover that local legends told of a worker in the Knox Building's early days named George who met an early doom when he plunged down an elevator shaft. His spirit was known to walk about the building at times and was, perhaps, the cause of some of the building's other hauntings like the sound of disembodied footsteps and doors opening and closing on their own.

The current staff has more to add to the legend as well. Sheet music randomly flies across the Palace of Versailles replica stage which cannot be explained by any draft in the building, and sometimes the aroma of cigar smoke wafts through the air of the smoke-free building. Does George not like the symphony, or is there more than one spirit that roams the structure? Taking in an event at the old Knox Building may be the only way to find out.

The Knox Building has served the Masons at different periods throughout its history.

Chapter Twenty-Four

Black Bear Church and Cemetery

Tucked away down a dirt road in Olive Township just southeast of Garber are the remnants of what many now call Black Bear Church and the adjacent Black Bear Cemetery. While the grounds of the burial site are well-kept, the church is a shell of its former self — crumbling and missing its roof, overgrown with vegetation, and graffiti-laden. It's hard to imagine that less than a hundred years ago it was a place where the local farmers gathered for worship, weddings, and funerals. Now, almost forgotten, it's a place where some come to desecrate and others come to investigate.

The cemetery was once known as the Baldwin Cemetery, named after the family that owned the property. Arthur D. Baldwin moved his family there from Missouri in 1896, just after the 1893 Cherokee Strip land run. His parcel of land was situated between two separate parcels owned by Richard Allen, and together, along with others in the community, Baldwin helped to build the New Bethany Baptist Church directly across the road from the cemetery plot.

Little is known about this small, out-of-the-way church. In 1942, New Bethany was awarded a $500 bond in a newspaper-sponsored scrap metal drive that nearly paid for all of their $693 debt. The forty-member church had collected 3,275 pounds of metal, but aside from that tidbit, and the eventual passing of the patrons, there is little information available. By 1972, New Bethany Baptist Church had disappeared from local maps and was a fading memory.

Abandoned, the building became an attractive haven for local teenagers and cult practitioners. Rumors swirled about what went on there and what might have happened in the church's unknown past. Did something diabolical happen at New Bethany in its waning days that caused it to close, or had trespassing witches conjured up something else with their black magic?

Paranormal teams are attracted to the area for the hotbed of energy that seems to emanate from the old church. Shadows morph out of the darkness and surround those who enter the forgotten sanctuary. Some have felt a force push them back as they near the basement and strange gusts of wind will suddenly kick up out of nowhere, knocking down equipment as they blow through. Voices and whispers are heard throughout, and it's not uncommon for cameras to pick up large balls of glowing light. Apparitions of the old local farmers are also seen.

The entrance of the old New Bethany Baptist Church in the dead of the night.

Footsteps and movement in the church are often heard, but this is not only relegated to the building. Sounds of someone stepping through the cemetery — and along the road — are also heard. On a personal visit to the location with Society of the Haunted members Cathy Nance and Logan Corelli, the three of us were about to enter Cathy's car and drive back over to the church (yes, it's directly across the street, but coyotes had been nearing us), but we paused when we heard the sound of heavy boots coming up the road toward us. It was very late at night, and we thought one of the locals had ventured out to see who was rustling through the cemetery shining flashlights and setting off flashbulbs. However, not a soul was there. The footsteps had been so loud that when we got in the car we actually drove up the road to find the person that had been walking. Again, there was no one.

A fantastic luminescent ball of light captured inside the Black Bear church.

Some late night visitors to Black Bear church have experienced more than they bargained for. Small shadow people, shorter than an average adult human, will creep out of the darkness and gather around those violating their grounds. They'll drive the visitors out, seemingly protecting the area from intruders. The stunted shadows have been known to scratch at car windows, throw objects inside of vehicles, and chase those driving away up the road to make sure they've completely left the ruins of the old church. Who or what they are no one knows for sure, but they are not soon forgotten.

Chapter Twenty-Five

Paranormal Kicks on Route 66

It was dark and dank, the roadbed still wet with rain that had poured down for hours. A mist hung in the air painting the aged sedan with fine droplets of water as the vehicle rambled down old Route 66. Up ahead on the right was a huddled figure in a brown trench coat and a tattered fedora trudging up the road. As the car neared, the driver determined that the figure seemed to be an older gentleman and slowed, taking pity upon the man and offering a ride out of the horrible weather. However, when the driver pulled up the figure disappeared into the mist.

The legendary Route 66, which ran its course through Illinois, Missouri, Kansas, Oklahoma, Texas, New Mexico, Arizona, and California is, arguably, the most famous historic highway in America. Named the "Mother Road" in John Steinbeck's 1939 novel *The Grapes of Wrath*, its origins grew to fruition in 1926 in the minds of Tulsa's Cyrus Avery and John Woodruff of Springfield, Missouri, who desired to connect Chicago and Los Angeles with a "super-highway"). It took the better part of a dozen years, but by 1938 the 2,300 mile highway was completed.

Following World War II, U.S. Route 66 became a symbol of American freedom, linking the two sides of the country together. Classic motels, diners, garages, and service stations sprouted up all along the highway to handle the influx of motorists. Roadside attractions such as small zoos, Indian curio shops, and sight-seeing locations also opened. "Get your kicks on Route 66" became a popular catchphrase after driving along this highway inspired songwriter Bobby Troup to write the song of that title, and was then recorded by Nat King Cole in 1946. The highway also saw the first fast-food restaurants with the first drive-through at Red Giant Hamburgs in Springfield, Missouri, and the first McDonald's in San Bernardino, California. The road itself was like a celebration of Americana.

However, the idea of a super-highway which began in 1926 and inspired the creation of Route 66, was also its demise. Most roads around the United States were narrow and fragmented, and not adequate for long distance travelling. President Dwight D. Eisenhower had seen the advancement of mobility in German roads when he was a general in World War II and set forth the building of America's vast interstate highway system in 1956. By 1970, most sections of Route 66 had been bypassed with new four-lane highways, and the final section was bypassed in 1984 in Williams, Arizona, with the completion of Interstate 40. The following year, U.S. Route 66 was officially decertified, and all that remained were a few strips of road scattered about the countryside.

Hitchhikers on Route 66 west of El Reno may not be of this world.

Interest in retaining segments of Route 66 has remained high and Oklahoma became the first state to design and install Historic Route 66 markers along the remaining sections of road. The country's first state-sponsored Route 66 museum was built in Clinton, Oklahoma. Tourism along these bits of road has increased, and a number of old service stations and diners have been restored as Americans seek out nostalgia. Perhaps that is why paranormal activity along The Mother Road has also increased.

The strip of Route 66 that runs from El Reno to Weatherford seems to be most particularly haunted. The visage of the old man on the roadside has a number of variations. As described above, some have tried to offer him a ride, but he will simply vanish into thin air. One person actually enticed him into the car and described him as an eerie little man. Suddenly, the man tried to jump out of the car after it started moving, so the driver pulled over to let him out. However, the man was no longer in the car and was not spotted anywhere nearby. A few miles down the road, the driver saw the gentleman walking along the roadside the same way as he had before. Other drivers have stated the apparition jumps out into the road and they think they've hit him, however, when they get out of their cars to check not a soul is around.

Scores of people have either been seriously injured or died in automobile accidents on this stretch of Route 66, including a 1952 wreck that claimed the lives of three people. In one strange mishap in nearly the same location, a man was tossed from the cab of a truck and died of severe chest injuries suffered from smacking the roadside. A 1953 collision just a few miles further west of El Reno during an intense downpour killed two and injured seven. It is said the creepy roadside vagabond is most often seen while it's raining. Is it possible he's a specter of one of these accidents?

Another specter that looms off a drive on Route 66 on the western outskirts of El Reno is Fort Reno, which served as an internment camp for more than 1,300 German and Italian POWs during World War II. Established during the Cheyenne uprising of 1874 to help protect the Cheyenne and Arapaho Indians, the fort was named for Union Civil War Major General Jesse L. Reno who died during the Battle of South Mountain in Maryland. Today, it is used as a research laboratory, and its historic section is a popular tourist attraction complete with re-enactors and ghost tours.

The Fort Reno Visitor's Center was once the Commandant's Quarters and is haunted by the spirit of Major Konat who committed suicide there in the 1930s after his wife left him. He's prone to changing the television channels and stomping about with his heavy combat boots. Both lights and faucets randomly turn themselves on and off as well. Occasionally, he will tap people on the shoulder and knock pictures off the walls.

The eerie military cemetery at the fort, where sixty-two German and eight Italian POWs are buried in the western end, has some strange tales associated with it. One German buried there, Hans Seifert, was due to be released, but the day before he was to be let go he accidentally killed himself by setting his body ablaze when lighting a gas stove. Johannes Kunze of the Tonkawa Camp was accused by his fellow prisoners of being a traitor and was beaten to death by many of them. Those that were charged with his murder were sent to Fort Leavenworth, Kansas, and were hung. Another strange tale is that of the funeral procession of a minister many years ago. His casket was being carried by a horse-drawn hearse one stormy day when the hearse was twice struck by lightning. Two of the four horses were killed and the minister was quickly buried before anything else happened.

U.S. Route 66 was part of the fabric of America for the better part of the twentieth century. It harkens back to a day when motorists could really experience and interact with the countryside and community instead of blowing past it on large, super-speed highways. With state governments and historic associations working to preserve the remnants of the Mother Road, you can still get your kicks on Route 66. Just be wary of picking up a huddled figure in a brown trench coat and a tattered fedora along the roadside.

The old Commandant quarters at Fort Reno where Major Konat committed suicide.

Chapter Twenty-Six

The Tragedies of Woodward

They're deadly, Oklahoma is known for them, and they used to come without any warning. A whirling cone of chaos, these intense storms can create pressure up to 1,000 pounds per square foot. Tornadoes are one of the most devastating forces on Earth, and the town of Woodward was flattened by the deadliest Oklahoman tornado on April 9, 1947.

There was virtually no warning. Three days into a national telephone strike, only emergency operators were working the switchboards and Woodward only had two shortly after 8:00 p.m. that fateful night when the call came in about the two-mile wide tornado that was ripping up the countryside. It had already leveled Glazier and Higgins, Texas, and Gale and Fargo, Oklahoma, but the first call from the Shattuck operator was to remark, "It's storming out here. Are you all right?"

Mrs. Grace Nix answering the board replied, "Yes, we're all right."

Moments later, the operator at Cestos to the southeast called. "There's a black cloud over Woodward. It looks terrible."

"I haven't had time to look," Grace responded, but ten minutes later every local number was lit on the board. Broken glass, tar paper from roofs, and pieces of awning began flying past the window and the switchboard went dead. Lightning blazed and wind roared like express trains rampaging the town.

There was almost no time to react. With electric lines starting to snap all around Woodward, Erwin Walker threw the master switch and killed the town's power, but a moment later the tornado ripped through the middle of the power plant and took Mr. Walker with it. The tornado roared on and devastated one hundred city blocks.

Residents witnessed walls separating from ceilings as windows imploded, porches and entire structures being ripped away, and a massive air conditioning unit blasting through the back door of the Terry Theater. Some that ran out into the streets were yanked off their feet and thrown across town like rag dolls to their deaths. Trees were ripped out of the ground and fires started by lightning broke out in the driving rain.

Tornadoes: one of the most destructive forces on Earth,
leaving devastation and death in its path.

Former U.S. District attorney Tom Hieronymus described the horror,
"There was lightning and thunder. It looks like a hard rain. Then all at once
my car wouldn't go anymore. It came to a complete stop and the engine
died. We could feel something beating on the car. I thought it was hail. We
sat there for five minutes. I rolled down the glass and looked out to see if
there was any damage. Not a house was standing, as far as I could see. Then
people came running from everywhere — bleeding, covered with mud, many
with hardly any clothes on — all crying for help. It was awful."

Franklin Stecher of the Armstrong Funeral Home remarked, "Two
minutes after the wind quieted, there was a knocking at the front door.
A car had overturned in the next block and two persons were hurt. We

started after them and have been going ever since. We could not pick up the dead. There were too many injured. The dead could not be moved until after midnight."

Volunteers began bringing the injured to Woodward Hospital and it quickly overfilled. The Baptist church was designated an emergency hospital, but it too was soon overflowing. Guests staying at the Baker Hotel were then moved out to make room for the injured, and other temporary hospitals were set up around what was left of the town as well. Woodward was in utter chaos with 107 dead.

In the basement of the Woodward Hospital, seven year-old Geraldine Croft sat with her four year-old sister Joan Gay as they awaited some word about the whereabouts of their parents. Their mother had been killed in the devastation, and their father, Olin, had been seriously injured. Joan had been pierced in the leg with a ten-inch splinter, but her injury was minor. A nurse came by and gave them some water. A little while later, two men in khakis approached the chubby-faced, adorable blond Joan and took her as if they were moving her to some other part of the hospital. She cried and said that she wanted to stay with her sister, but they continued on and Joan Gay Croft was never seen again.

Olin recovered and began a never-ending search for his daughter. A multi-state investigation was started several months later, but it proved fruitless. Olin and Geraldine left Woodward and continued their search elsewhere.

Years later, a 1993 episode of *Unsolved Mysteries* featuring Joan Gay prompted a number of women with mysterious pasts to suspect that they may be the missing Woodward girl. The family was so sure about one particular woman that they were in the process of welcoming her into the family when a DNA test proved otherwise. More than sixty years later, Joan Gay Croft is still missing since her abduction from the bowels of Woodward Hospital during a night of horrific tragedy. She may be someone's beloved grandmother out there completely oblivious to her true origins.

There are three other mysterious victims from the tornado devastation. Three young girls, ages eight months, three or four years old, and twelve years old were never identified. Authorities claimed to have used every identification method possible to try and discover who the girls may be. Every school teacher in Woodward came to the morgue with their enrollment books to check it against the identity of the deceased. Then the opposite was tried — they took every name in their books and traced them back. Everyone in their books were accounted for. Some people suspect that the girls may be children of transients passing through the area that couldn't afford burial. Others think the girls may be victims from other towns whose bodies got caught up in the tornado and were dropped into Woodward. In 1997, a memorial was erected at the middle school honoring all the young victims of the tornado.

The natural disaster acted as a catalyst for a couple of different changes. First, because of the lack of communication and a more timely warning given to the citizens of the area, the National Weather Service implemented its tornado watch and warning program in 1953. Secondly, while plans for a new hospital in Woodward were already underway, the disaster helped to expedite the process and a new facility was erected in 1952.

The original hospital was built as a private residence in the early 1900s and was converted to a small hospital in 1912. For forty years it served Woodward well as a venue of life and death, but the town outgrew the antiquated facility. It is now a dilapidated piece of architecture with nothing but its memories, mysteries, and ghosts remaining.

The most common haunting associated with Woodward Hospital is that of a little girl who is known to be playful. People passing by have seen a young girl's face peeking through the remaining windows, prompting them to enter and investigate. Inside, a shadow of a young child has been seen in the hallways accompanied with giggling, and it's believed that this is the same girl that has been seen in the windows. At times the giggling is disembodied and other unexplainable noises have been heard throughout. She may be playing some sort of hide-and-seek game with visitors that venture inside. Most people do not believe this is the spirit of Joan Gay Croft. This child spirit appears to be older than four years of age, and it's widely believed that Joan Gay was extradited far from the hospital. She may even still be alive.

Other incidents have been reported in the old hospital as well. Strange flashing lights have been seen and other disembodied voices have been heard whispering throughout the decrepit walls. Paranormal teams that have investigated the structure have recorded strange temperature fluctuations, at times dropping more than ten degrees in just five minutes. Slamming doors and loud knocks have also been witnessed.

The old Woodward Hospital is an interesting piece of history, having survived the devastating tornado in 1947 and housing much of the ensuing chaos. Tragedy has accompanied it, but while a little girl was taken away from it in life, it seems one has been added to it in death.

Part 6

Southwest Oklahoma

Chapter Twenty-Seven
Geronimo and Fort Sill

The crash of thunder startled her comatose body out of its repose. It was 2 a.m., hours into a long, listless sleep, but a storm blowing through the area shocked her system into alert mode. She stumbled out of bed to make sure all the windows were secured shut and the house was prepared for a possible power outage. Half grumbling, she staggered into the living room and reached for one of the windows — and that's when she saw it.

A flash of lightning flooded the entire Old Post Quadrangle with bright, white light except for one specific spot. From the large tree outside of her quarters she saw a man strung up in a noose, limp and seemingly dead. She rushed back to the bedroom and shook her husband awake, exclaiming, "Come quick! Someone hung himself from the tree out front!"

They grabbed flashlights and ran outside, but when they got there the man was gone. They examined the area for any possible sign of him — a piece of rope, a piece of clothing — but nothing was found. They chalked up the incident to an odd lighting effect caused by the lightning and the tree. However, it wasn't long before they heard a similar account from another family on post that had seen the same thing. And not long after that they'd heard that the same image of a man hanging from the tree had been reported during a storm a few years prior.

This is just one of the ghost tales that is associated with historic Fort Sill, home of the U.S. Army's Field Artillery. Ft. Sill's origins dates back to the mid-1800s in a region that was frequented by early U.S. military expeditions and where President Sam Houston of the Republic of Texas sent emissaries to negotiate a treaty with the Comanche Indians in order to halt their raids into his territory. In 1951, three years after the Mexican-American War, Capt. Randolph B. Marcy named Mount Scott after General Winfield Scott, a hero from that conflict, and suggested that a fort be built in that area. It wasn't until after the Civil War that a post, Camp Wichita, was built there in 1868, and a year later expanded into a full-fledged military installation named Fort Sill after Brigadier General Joshua W. Sill who had been killed at the battle of Stones River, Tennessee, in 1862.

Are all bones present and accounted for in Geronimo's grave?
Courtesy of Cathy Nance.

Fort Sill is notorious for its Apache prisoner of war camp, which was established in 1894 when Geronimo and 341 other Chiricahua Apache Indians were extradited from the Mount Vernon Barracks in Alabama. In Oklahoma they lived in small camps that were scattered about the post until 1913 when they either moved onto the Mescalero Apache Reservation or parcels of land around Fletcher and Apache. They are now known as the Fort Sill Apache Tribe.

On February 17, 1909, Geronimo died of pneumonia after being thrown from his horse and spending an entire night out in the cold while awaiting help. He was buried at the Fort Sill Apache Prisoner of War Cemetery. It has been believed by some that members of the Skull and Bones secret society at Yale University stole Geronimo's skull, a few other bones, and some of his personal effects from the cemetery and placed them in the society's own tomb. However, the claims have been consistently refuted.

Skull and Bones member Winter Mead wrote in a letter in 1918, "The skull of the worthy Geronimo the Terrible, exhumed from its tomb at Fort Sill by your club and the Knight Haffner, is now safe inside the Tomb together with his well worn femurs, bit and saddle horn."

The problem with this claim is that Mead was never at Fort Sill. Some believe that if the Bonesmen did rob a grave then they may have stolen bones from the wrong Indian since Geronimo's grave was not marked at the time.

The Geronimo Acres housing area on the Army post has been the center of much of the fort's paranormal activity. Tenants have reported strange occurrences of hair pulling, poking, smacking, beds being kicked or shaken, and animals staring at and reacting to things that aren't there. Various types of apparitions have been spotted including Indian children playing out in the yard, mists forming in rooms, and full-bodied soldiers walking through houses. While the housing area is not near a cemetery, many people have attributed the activity to the number of unmarked graves that are scattered about the fort.

Back at the Old Post Quadrangle, repairs were being made in the more than 100-year-old officers' quarters. The workers consistently heard someone running around upstairs, but any time they went to see who may have been there they discovered no one. The local legend is that they completed the job in record time and got out of there as quickly as possible. Those that are stationed at Fort Sill don't have that luxury.

Chapter Twenty-Eight

Riverside Indian School

The Riverside Indian School is the oldest federally operated American Indian boarding school in the country and is located in Anadarko. Prior to its current location along the Washita River, it was organized in 1871 at the old Wichita Indian Agency commissary and in 1872 it became the Wichita-Caddo School. By the late 1870s the school was shifted to its current location and renamed the Riverside Indian School.

As other schools of its kind closed, Riverside began accommodating more students, beginning with the Kiowa that began enrolling there in 1922 and the Navajos in 1945. Currently, the school teaches student from dozens of different Indian tribes in grades four through twelve.

It seems that the haunting at Riverside Indian School is a relatively mild one, but still unsettling enough to those that attend there. The most common report is that of voices throughout the campus, echoes of Native American students from long ago talking in their native tongue. Sometimes these voices are even heard to be singing and are occasionally accompanied by the beat of a drum.

Some of the ghost stories have filtered out from specific dormitories over the years. In one room in the Araphao dorm, a ghostly hand has been seen rapping against a window while in the Delaware dorm doors have opened and closed on their own and objects have gone missing or are oddly misplaced. The apparition of a ghostly girl has been seen in the Cheyenne dormitory, seeming so life-like that an attending girl thought she was still talking to her friend that had been in the room with her just moments before. When she realized she was actually talking to a ghost she started screaming and ran down the hall.

The apparition that is seen most often at Riverside Indian School is that of a morbid young boy. He is commonly seen with bruises on his face as if he's been beaten or was in some sort of fight. He is Native American and some have said he wears an old school uniform. The boy doesn't interact with anyone, although he is likely not a residual haunting. He is seen in different areas of the campus, will stare at people and walk off, and sometimes will just stare and disappear.

There had been the tragic death of a boy at Riverside back in 1949 when he, his brother, and a friend were swimming at nearby Shirley Springs. The boy was wading and slipped fourteen feet into a deep hole of the cold spring. He was never seen alive again, his body eventually pulled out by a local baseball player. Could this possibly be the boy seen around campus and the marks on his face a sign of his horrific end? At this point we don't know.

Native American school children in the early 1900s.
Courtesy of the Yale Collection of Western Americana.

Chapter Twenty-Nine

Robbery Gone Awry in Waurika

The Rock Island Railroad had its beginnings in 1845 when James Grant wanted to connect the Mississippi River port of Rock Island to the Illinois & Michigan Canal in La Salle, Illinois. When Grant's vision expanded westward, the Rock Island Railroad became credited with constructing the first man-made bridge over the Mississippi in 1856. This new structure wasn't without its controversies when shortly after it was built a steamboat crashed into it. Its continued operation was challenged in court, but a lawyer for Rock Island, future president Abraham Lincoln, successfully saved the bridge and the construction of future bridges. Lincoln also patented a device to buoy vessels over shoals and remains the only president to have held a patent.

By the 1880s, the moniker "Pacific" was added to the title of the railroad and a line to Colorado Springs was completed in 1888. Track rights to Denver were acquired in 1889, a connection with the Southern Pacific a few years later, and by the mid-1890s Rock Island was concentrating on building south through the new developing territory in Oklahoma.

The town of Waurika was established on the 98th Meridian in 1901, and shortly thereafter the Rock Island Railroad connected through, designating Waurika as a flag station. To accommodate travelers, a boarding house and restaurant known as the Rock Island Rooming House was constructed alongside the tracks.

In the early days of the boarding house, a robber paraded in to the dining room with his pistol and tried to hold up everyone who was there. The burly railroad men staying there that night were going to have none of it and overwhelmed the perpetrator. In a surprise to everyone there, the robber actually died in the struggle. The railroad workers didn't want to get in trouble, so they quickly loaded the body aboard one of the boxcars and walked away from the scene. The train left the station with the murdered man stowed away. Others further up the line found the body aboard the train and buried the robber in an unmarked grave.

The boarding house later became the Moneka Mall and Tea Room and is now Nancy's Antiques. Many of the strange occurrences that happen there are attributed to the spirit of the man who tried to rob the patrons of the old restaurant over one hundred years ago. Most of the haunts occur on the north and east sides on all floors and have become more prevalent since the recent remodel to Nancy's Antiques. People feel a distinct chill when they enter the shop, as if they're crossing the threshold into the other side of the veil. Disembodied voices and footsteps are heard throughout, and old typewriters have begun operating on their own. One story from nearly twenty years ago tells how the proprietor would walk out to her car at night after turning the lights out in the building only to find that the lights had been turned back on. The old robber may have had an unsuccessful criminal career, but thus far he's been a pretty successful ghost.

The railroad played an influential role in Oklahoma's development...
as well as in some of its ghost stories.

Chapter Thirty

The "Leave or Die" House

It's a story that makes your skin crawl. While many people are unsure whether or not they believe in ghosts, they are more apt to believe in the existence of demons. Perhaps it is because of the belief most people have in a higher power and its influence that they also believe in a lower power and its influence. Evil exists in many forms in this world, but it becomes much more frightening when it's a part of the spiritual world that comes forth unseen and malevolent. When a family moved into a house in Eldorado, Oklahoma, and saw the words "Leave or Die" painted on it, they didn't think it could have been a reference to this malevolence. It was probably just some mischievous kids and their graffiti, right?

The house was originally the Missionary Baptist Church which opened on June 27, 1906, during Eldorado's infancy. While the post office was established in the area in 1890, the actual town site of Eldorado shifted about for more than a decade until the St. Louis and San Francisco Railway line was built through and the town was permanently settled to take advantage of it. Eldorado was officially incorporated in 1904, just seven miles from the Red River and the border of Texas.

On July 18, 1902, the town's first newspaper, *The Eldorado Light*, provided an interesting summary of the town's religious beginnings, albeit littered with English errors: "As to the first church organizer your writer has no data, but the Baptist and Methodist were almost contemporaneous [sic]. Among the early ministers was Re. Lowther (Baptist) and Jas. Kizziar (Methodist). ... In the early days the Eldorado community was noted for its morality and when your writer first settled here there were thirty-five grown young ladies fifty young men nearly all of whom belonged to the church and although there were citizens from nearly every state in the union it was a remark frequently made that 'This is the best community I ever lived in.'"

After the Missionary Baptist Church served its time as a parish for forty-four years, it became a private residence. Curiously, in more recent years the house has had new owners more frequently than it did in the past. The family that bought the house in September, 1977, only lived there for a year and nine months while one family that bought the house in 1979 only lived there for eleven days. There was also a fourteen-year period in which the home was used as a rental and no family remained there longer than two years. Some answers about the families' short stays starting coming to light when the Solis family bought the house with "Leave or Die" painted upon it in December 2007; their experiences were featured in an episode of *The Haunted* on Animal Planet.

As soon as Ron, Gloria, and their daughter moved into the home, one of the family's mini- Chihuahuas fell ill and died. The television show only shows one, Pongo, but there had been a second and it was buried in the backyard with a small cross erected as a grave marker. This cross is shown many times throughout the episode, but it was never made clear why it was there.

One of the first incidents that happened to the family in the home was also not reported on *The Haunted* and occurred during some restoration work in the older kitchen (the church and the parsonage had been combined into one single dwelling, providing two kitchens). While the Solis's were peeling paint they were suddenly attacked by a swarm of flies that filled the kitchen. Frantically, they found a can of Raid and sprayed the flies, but instead of falling dead to the floor they simply disappeared into thin air. The family was baffled by the disappearance of the pests and could not figure out how the flies entered the home in the first place since no windows or doors had been opened.

During this time, Pongo, who had always been very active, had suddenly become a despondent animal that would stare off at something unseen for long periods of time, almost as if in a trance. After the trance would break, he would then become very nervous and skittish. After a few weeks in the home, Pongo started losing his hair and the veterinarian could not find any cause for it. Shortly after this began, as the season neared Christmas, the dog began barking wildly at something unseen in the kitchen. Gloria went in to take a look and heard a deep, intense growl that could not have come from her small mini-Chihuahua. Startled, Gloria thought a large dog had entered the home, but no large dog was present inside or outside the residence.

Two weeks later, Pongo was in bed with Ron and Gloria while they were sleeping when the dog suddenly started barking and growling at something in the room. Ron woke up to see what was going on and felt his head burning. Shocked, his wife saw that he was losing his hair in clumps. At the same time, Roy noticed Gloria had markings on her forehead that resembled a cross. They frantically started searching the house for intruders, someone that may have snuck into their room and violated them, but they found no one and the entire house was locked tight.

Upset and desperate for answers, Gloria tracked down the previous owners of the home who had only lived there a year and a half. Their son was willing to share that he had heard voices in the house — a couple children and a man — although he never saw *who* was talking or where they were coming from.

With all the strange occurrences in the home and now a story about voices from the previous owners, Gloria reached out to Oklahoma Paranormal Research and Investigations (OKPRI). During their initial sweep of the home, the team recorded a

Formerly a church, the house in Eldorado has since become something sinister. *Courtesy of Cathy Nance.*

number of high electromagnetic field (EMF) spikes as they investigated the structure. Numerous electronic voice phenomena (EVPs) captured during audio recording sessions were quite foreboding and included, "Get out," "Bite me, bite me, bite me," and, "You will die today."

During the investigation, OKPRI founder Christy Clark began feeling ill, so she and three other team members went outside to get some air. Christy continued to worsen, nearly passed out, and started getting hostile toward the other members. She suddenly felt a desire to choke someone and began to feel as if she were under a spiritual attack.

One of the other investigators boldly stepped forward and stated, "Back off her or I'm going to deal with you." At that remark, the spirit that was aggravating Christy turned and knocked this investigator straight to the ground. For four full minutes she was in a fit with mutterings and growls in a voice that was not her own. The investigator later described that it felt like her face was on fire.

Christy recounted the scene, "The moment she hit the ground I jumped to her side and tried to help her up, but she appeared unconscious and every muscle in her body was stiff as a board, and she couldn't be moved. I then immediately heard growling coming out of her mouth and I began rebuking the entity I knew that had gained entrance into her body. The more I rebuked the entity and told it to leave, snickering would come out of her mouth as if to mock and laugh at us. She also spoke a few words that were in a language I did not understand nor did any of my other team members."

Investigator and theologian Chris Borthick who was present at the scene confirmed, "She started muttering and growling and saying things in a voice that was clearly not hers. I thought the thing was a demon."

After the frightening incident, the stricken investigator said she felt angry and violated by the spirit and subsequently left OKPRI.

After the possession incident, the Solis family temporarily moved in with Gloria's mother, but it was not a long-term solution. Although everyone felt a weight lift off their shoulders, and even Pongo showed signs of improvement, the family had to return to the old church. They put the house on the market, but there were no offers so they were trying to make the best of their situation while living in the home. They couldn't afford to try and rent or buy another house elsewhere.

OKPRI returned to the house in Eldorado with renowned demonologist, Carl Johnson, to perform a cleansing of the residence. Of interest to Johnson were the markings which Gloria had incurred on her face and the guttural voice that emanated from the OKPRI investigator. They began a circle of prayer during which Gloria began to feel overwhelmed. Gloria soon recovered and Carl proceeded to bless the house with holy water and anointing oil with the assistance of OKPRI case manager, Cathy Nance. The blessing then moved into the backyard where shadows scurried away from the house, many climbing into the trees. Some there also thought they heard the name "Baal" called out into the dark night. Carl was confident that he had rid the house of its demons that night, but was sure the Solis's were going to be challenged for some time afterward.

The Solis family has since moved out of the home.

Is what has happened in the home a desecration of the good that had once resided there? The building had been a church and the spirit of God once filled its rooms, but after the parishioners had left did something sinister enter its confines in order to mock what had previously been? It's possible, but at this point it would be pure speculation.

The town of Eldorado is built over gypsum beds, and for a time was the home of the Unites States Gypsum Company. Gyps is Greek for "burned mineral" and the composition of gypsum is part sulfur, however, white gypsum was also used by ancient priestesses to paint their faces for purification and to emulate the goddesses of light. The contrast is evident, with the sulfur often regarded as the scent of Satan while it and its derivatives have also been used for healing and purification. Likewise is the contrast with the Eldorado house, once a church but now seemingly the den of the devil.

Part 7

Other Oklahoma Haunts

Chapter Thirty-One
Cemeteries

For centuries there has been an attraction toward cemeteries for varying reasons. In modern times, unfortunately, one of those reasons is that teens routinely like to enter them at night for small parties and dares. They see cemeteries as a spooky thrill and have made it difficult for paranormal investigators to enter burial grounds at night. Burial grounds are often closed at night with after dark rules placed into effect and police keeping them under surveillance. Researchers, historians, and genealogists appreciate the history cemeteries contain and the family records therein that are carved in stone. Grandchildren of generations past are thankful that they have a place they can go to trace their family roots and see physical evidence of their family's legacy. Some go to admire the elaborate carvings on the headstones, including sculpted angels, flowers, or the magnificently carved "logs" of the Woodmen of the World headstones. Also, paranormal investigators have found many cemeteries to be quite spiritually active for recording evidence of paranormal existence.

Cemeteries in Oklahoma have an interesting and colorful history. Some were once segregated, some belong to a town that no longer exists, some started off as a family plot that was extended to include the local community, some belong to churches, and then there are Indian Burial Grounds, the locations of which many are unknown.

A common question about haunted cemeteries is, "If spirits haunt places because of their memories of a location or object, then why are they at the cemetery?" There are a few theories about this. One is that the entity has become attached to his or her body. Another is that the object to which he or she is attached may also be buried in the casket with the corpse. The cemetery may have guardian spirits watching over it, appointed caretakers of the dead. Many spirits are transient and are just "passing through" without a real connection to the cemetery or people there. Other hauntings could be residual energy playing itself over. Given the grieving that occurs at such places, this mark can certainly be made.

A fantastic sculpted Woodmen of the
World headstone at Retrop Cemetery.

One such tale is that of a female spirit at the Fort Gibson cemetery. Her fiancé had abandoned her at the altar, but she tracked him down to the frontier fort in the late 1800s. Desperate to know what was going on, she disguised herself as a man and served in the military on post near him. She began following him home at nights and discovered that he was taking up with a Native American woman who lived nearby. Bitter and enraged, she confronted the man one night and murdered him with a shotgun. After he was buried, she resented what she had done and longed for her former fiancé to be alive again. She started visiting his grave at night and crying herself to sleep on his headstone. One frigid evening she froze to death on his headstone, but her spirit has continued to visit the grave.

Some believe that cemeteries make excellent locations for portals, although portals could be located almost anywhere. A portal is believed to be an opening between dimensions or spiritual worlds in which spirits are able to freely pass through and go elsewhere. Years ago, Christy Clark of OKRPI captured a fantastic photograph of a possible portal at one of the Earlsboro cemeteries, but has yet to capture the anomaly again. It could be an indicator that portals can become closed or are only opened at certain times.

Another interesting capture she acquired on digital camera is that of what looks like a flame rising from the ground near a headstone at Romulus Cemetery. The town of Romulus no longer exists and the area is considered an unincorporated community, but those that once lived and attended school there still make their presence known. During that same investigation, there were a number of fluctuations and spikes on the gaussmeter, especially in the southeast corner.

There are a number of cemeteries throughout Oklahoma that contain noteworthy headstones of outlaws and such forgotten souls that the markers don't even give them a proper name. Both of these are the case at Dick Duck Cemetery in Catoosa. Although the land was donated by Richard Duck in the early 1800s, it's a Duck of a different name that has made this cemetery distinguished.

A "Half Breed" marker at Dick Duck Cemetery.

Bluford "Blue" Duck, whose Cherokee name was Sha-con-gah Kaw-wan-nu, was riding drunk one evening with William Christie when they came upon a young man named Samuel Wyrick and Duck suddenly unloaded his entire revolver into the man. He then reloaded and fired at a nearby Indian boy who had leapt up on a horse to go get help. Duck was tracked down and arrested. It's unknown whether Blue truly knew female outlaw Belle Starr, but there is a story that circulated which stated that prior to Belle's marriage to Sam Starr, Blue and Belle had a short affair, and it is due to this affair that Belle assisted with Blue's appeal after he had been sentenced to hang. What is known for sure is that a picture of Blue and Belle was taken at that time, and Blue's sentence was changed to life in prison in 1886. Nine years later, Duck grew deathly ill, and with one month to live, President Grover Cleveland pardoned the outlaw so he could spend that final month with family and friends. Bluford Duck was buried at Dick Duck Cemetery on May 7, 1895.

In what seems to be a sign of the times in the 1880s around the Catoosa area near Tulsa, there is a series of small white headstones within Dick Duck Cemetery that have been marked as "Half Breed." Not much is known about these markers, all dated between 1882 and 1883, but they eerily speak out to us about the culture of America at that time.

Other tragedies are present at Arapaho Cemetery in the western part of the state. Buried there is Robina Smith whose grave is visited by many who seek out her legend. As a young nineteen-year-old woman in 1936, Robina was killed in a horrific car accident with a creamery truck. Her father was grief-stricken over the fact that his daughter had not yet sought salvation from God, and he feared for her fate in the afterlife. Following his death in 1972, visitors to the cemetery began hearing a voice near Robina's grave crying out, "Oh Lord, my God, Robina has not yet been saved." This cry has been known to interrupt funeral services at Arapaho, and when a geologist studied the site to determine a natural cause for the voice he couldn't find one and even heard the voice himself.

Lima Cemetery was a short side investigation we had made while the team was still together with OKPRI. Following a regular residential investigation, we stopped by to see what type of activity happened at the cemetery since we had recently heard some interesting stories about the location. On the way there, our psychic, Christy Clark, felt nauseous and was getting sick. On the way there, our psychic, Christy Clark, felt nauseous and was getting sick. When we reached the cemetery, Chris Borthick also felt uneasy and elected to stay and watch over Christy while the rest of us ventured into the graveyard. We picked up a few EVPs such as, "You go around me," and, "Do not go down there," but there was one I caught near the end of our visit that piqued my attention.

The legendary gravesite of Robina Smith where the ghost of her father still mourns.

We had just closed the cemetery gate and were getting ready to leave, when I wandered over to the fence to take a final few pictures. I was standing next to an old stone pillar that constituted part of the fence when Christy suddenly called out to me that on the right side of the pillar she saw a spirit. I couldn't see it, but I decided to be polite and introduce myself, "Hi, how are you? I'm Michael."

My audio recorder picked up a male voice that replied, "Edward."

To top it off, as we were piling into the cars, three large dogs came bounding up the road like hellhounds, which told us that we had overstayed our welcome.

These are but a few tales of cemeteries around the state of Oklahoma. There are hundreds scattered about the landscape with their own historic and eerie tales to tell. Why do the spirits linger there? They seem to each have their own reasons.

Chapter Thirty-Two
Ghost Towns

Oklahoma is littered with a multitude of ghost towns and abandoned frontier locales. That's not to mean Oklahoma is a dying state. On the contrary, Oklahoma's population rose 6.9% between 2000 and 2009, they just landed their own NBA team in the Thunder, and Oklahoma City's MAPS (Metropolitan Area Projects) initiative has driven business back downtown while creating a viable tourist attraction. However, the state's formative years saw many small towns sprout up only to dwindle away for a variety of reasons, including railroad placement, oil boomtowns running dry, and The Great Depression. Some of these towns still have structures standing while others are only remembered by the local cemetery that remains as a specter of the past.

So what exactly is a ghost town? There is no precise definition for what one is, and it is really up to the discretion of the writer of the subject to determine how much of a percentage of its population a town has lost before he or she will classify it as a ghost town. In 1978, John W. Morris published *Ghost Towns of Oklahoma*, which is still the most comprehensive book about Oklahoman ghost towns to date. The criteria he used was, "hamlets, villages, towns, and cities (1) that are no longer in existence, all buildings and indications of existence having been either destroyed or covered by water; (2) where the remains of business and/or residential structures still stand but are largely unused; and (3) where, in the case of larger places, the population has decreased at least eighty percent from its maximum."

I don't plan to cover anywhere near as much material as Morris (he covered 130 different towns). If you are really quite interested in ghost towns, then I highly suggest his book, which is loaded with dozens of historic photographs, but I have adhered to his standard for my coverage in this work.

Earlsboro, with its colorful history, is a classic example of a boomtown that dried up and is but a shadow of its former self. The town actually had two booms. The first was a whiskey boom near the turn of the twentieth century since liquor was prohibited in Indian Territory but legal in Oklahoma Territory, and Earlsboro's close proximity to Indian Territory made it a haven of saloons. At one point, nearly 80% of Earlsboro's economy was derived from alcohol. A blacksmith shop, gristmill, and cotton gin were also installed, and as more people moved in churches were started, a school district was organized, and the railroad started servicing the town.

A few crumbling buildings are all that's left of Earlsboro's bustling Main Street.

The second was an oil boom in 1926 when black gold was struck and the oil derricks moved in. At this, Earlsboro's population soared to over 10,000 people within a short couple months, and construction took off. Main Street was lengthened to accommodate a number of new commercial buildings including stores, pool halls, beauty shops, cafes, a lumberyard, and a new four-story brick hotel. Professionals of all types, such as doctors, lawyers, and engineers, moved in to town, and shotgun houses and tents sprouted up all over.

This instant growth created quite a problem for Earlsboro since it didn't have the infrastructure to support the new populace. There was no sewage disposal, roads were unpaved and the new heavy traffic patterns kicked up dust everywhere, the small rail depot lacked the track and storage space that became required, and the post office was completely inadequate to handle the heavy quantities of mail. Since Earlsboro had no delivery service at that time, people lined up around the block to pick up their mail from the delivery window.

This settled down by 1928 as the boom subsided, and those that had come to make a quick buck in oil departed. By 1930, the population had already dwindled down to 1,950, and it continued to shrink over the decades to a few hundred. Over the years, however, this has included a number of colorful characters. Hall of Fame baseball player, Willie Stargell, was born in Earlsboro, as was Ernest McFarland who served as a U.S. Senator in Arizona from 1941 to 1953, and later as its governor from 1955 to 1959. Earlsboro was also a favorite stomping ground of the outlaw "Pretty Boy" Floyd.

Charles Arthur Floyd, called "Pretty Boy" by his prostitute girlfriend Beulah Baird "Juanita" Ash, but known as Charley or Choc to his friends, was a notorious Midwest bank robber in the 1920s and early 1930s. He served three and a half years at the Missouri State Penitentiary and had been sentenced to fifteen years at the Ohio State Penitentiary on a murder charge, but he escaped on the way there by leaping from a moving train. He made for Oklahoma, and Floyd actually spent some time working the oil fields near Earlsboro where Floyd's brother Bradley lived, but he generally stayed on the move.

In 1931, he teamed with George Birdwell of Irish, Cherokee, and Choctaw descent, and together they robbed thirteen banks, although they were accused of more. Their first target was the Bank of Earlsboro, which they robbed on March 9, hauling in $3,000. Encouraged, they went on to hold up banks in Shamrock, Morris, and Maud, two of which are now also ghost towns. The day following the Maud robbery, Floyd and Birdwell were confronted by law officers near Sallisaw, but sped away in their car after a short gunfight. A month later, on October 14, they hit Earlsboro again, bringing in a little less than their first hit at $2,500.

Despite the havoc he ensued upon the local towns, Floyd was always generous with his friends and family. One of his nephews in Earlsboro recalled always enjoying Uncle Charley's visits to their house. "He'd take me places with him, and when we were driving down those country roads, he'd let me drive that old Model T car."

Even some of the locals in Earlsboro had fond memories of Floyd, and he preferred being known as the "Robin Hood of the Cookson Hills." A woman who had been a teenager in the 1930s recalled an experience with Pretty Boy at the local drugstore where she and her brother had bought nickel ice cream cones. "One afternoon we were sitting there with our cones and in walks Pretty Boy Floyd. Everybody was buzzing about him. He was so handsome! His clothes were neat and he wore gloves. He ordered himself a Coca-Cola® and drank it down, and as he turned to leave he gave us a wink. Well, we were ready to leave, too, and when we went to pay for our ice cream, we found out he had already taken care of it for us."

One incident seemed more like a candid Hollywood moment when Floyd and Birdwell grabbed the local Earlsboro marshal on his way to work at the lumberyard, believing he was a private detective trying to snuff out the bandits' hideout. They drove him out to the country and began beating him, but once the marshal explained who he was the beating stopped and the duo profusely apologized for their mistake. Floyd even gave their victim a wad of cash to go get help from a doctor.

After a shootout in Bixby, the hometown of Floyd's ex-wife and son, left McIntosh County Sheriff Erv Kelley dead, the price on Floyd's head skyrocketed. Scores of law officers descended up Bixby and Earlsboro, but that did not stop Floyd and Birdwell from infiltrating Earlsboro when Birdwell's father died in the spring of 1932. It must have been quite a sight in the funeral home as Birdwell viewed his father and paid his respects with Floyd guarding the entrance with a submachine gun.

Although officers did not come after them at the mortuary, Earlsboro was no longer a safe haven for them. When the local Chief of Police discovered their car, he had it impounded; however, Floyd approached the Chief's home using a local African American as a human shield and forced the Chief to return the car. Floyd and Birdwell fled and what became known as "the most intensive manhunt Oklahoma has seen since the days of Al Jennings and the Dalton Brothers" ensued.

The duo were in and out of the state and reports of their whereabouts came from all over as bank robberies increased, with Floyd usually getting the credit whether he was truly involved or not. Birdwell was killed in Boley, Oklahoma, during a botched bank job that involved $50,000.

Pretty Boy Floyd and new partner Adam Richetti became the primary suspects of a gunfight that was known as the "Kansas City massacre" in which four law officers were gunned down on June 17, 1933. Floyd denied he was ever a part of the fight, and there is still controversy to this day as to whether or not he was a participant. On the run by the FBI for over a year, Charles Arthur Floyd was killed in a cornfield near East Liverpool, Ohio, on October 22, 1934. There are number of conflicting stories by the FBI agents that were present as to how the battle and Floyd's death truly happened.

Earlsboro no longer resembles the town Pretty Boy Floyd often visited. Few of its Main Street structures remain from that time, the hotel burned down ages ago, and the old drugstore where Floyd would buy ice creams for local kids is long since gone. Also lingering is a tiny service station from the 1940s that is used as little more than a storage shed for hay. The train doesn't even stop at the town anymore, but some say they've seen the apparition of an old railroad worker patrolling the grounds and humming a tune. And on a still night when all is quiet, you may yet hear Choc Floyd and George Birdwell revisiting their old stomping grounds.

Frisco and Reno City are two towns that met with the same fate due to their placement in relation to the North Canadian River. Frisco was platted just before the opening of the Unassigned Lands in 1889 north of the river and was also known as Veteran City since it was settled largely by group of Civil War veterans. It had been a thriving small town seemingly headed in the right direction with approximately 1,000 citizens eagerly anticipating the arrival of the railroad. It was home to a cotton gin, saw mill, two print shops, and numerous stores. The Oklahoma Frisco College was established in the town, and the first Grand Army of the Republic post was placed in Frisco. With its prominence, Frisco won the popular vote for the location of the county seat, but through political wrangling El Reno stole the honor.

All that remains of Frisco is its cemetery.

For a brief period of time, Reno City was the third largest town in Oklahoma Territory, boasting a population between 1,500 and 2,000 persons. Also established in 1889 north of the North Canadian River, it housed a flour and feed mill, four blacksmiths, two livery stables, two barber shops, a hotel, and fifteen other stores. At one point three different newspapers were in publication at Reno City.

When the Choctaw, Oklahoma, and Gulf Railroad began building westward, they wanted the town of Reno City to pay $40,000 or divide their real estate holdings in order to secure the railroad's placement in their town. Local residents scoffed at this proposal, believing that the railroad was bluffing and there was no way CO&G would pass up building through their prominently established site. Without the money from Reno City, CO&G instead placed their tracks south of the North Canadian River and established El Reno. There was still a chance for Reno City to acquire a railroad when the Chicago, Kansas, and Nebraska Railroad built southward out of Kansas, but they built through a deep ravine to the west and also connected to El Reno.

With the hopes of their town's future dashed, residents of Reno City packed up and moved south across the river, even taking some of their buildings with them. The hotel was actually stranded on the river for a few days. Today, there is nothing left of Reno City except for a foundation or two lost in the fields.

This political outmaneuvering by the railroad likewise destroyed Frisco. Also being located north of the river and awaiting the railroad to pass through, the citizens of Frisco did much the same as their brethren in Reno City. They packed up their belongings and many of their buildings, and set forth across the river to establish Yukon five miles to the south. For a long time the streets and alleys of Frisco remained, but in 1968 a farmer wanted to plow and plant the area and a decree was sought for the vacating of a portion of the plat of Frisco since it remained within the limits of Yukon, although unused. Today, the ghosts of Frisco's past may only be visited at the Frisco Cemetery, the last remnant of the old frontier town.

Some ghost towns were prominent enough that they were formerly county seats. Cloud Chief, originally called Tacola, had been the seat of H County, now Washita County. Streets and blocks had already been laid out before the town was even established because it was designated to be the county seat prior to the 1892 Cheyenne and Arapaho land run. Within two hours of the opening, a tent city sprouted up complete with stores, saloons, and gambling dens. This was short-lived, however, as settlers had only six months from filing their claim to go settle, and transportation facilities in Cloud Chief were nearly non-existent. The town muddled about until 1893 when a sawmill was built, bringing with it renewed commerce. By 1898, the town had grown up enough where it housed two hardware stores, two restaurants, two grocery stores, two saloons, a blacksmith, a barbershop, a livery stable, a hotel, and a print shop for the county newspaper.

Even with business growing in Cloud Chief, residents in the western and central part of the county petitioned the County Commissioner to move the seat to Cordell. Legal battles erupted, and soon an election was designated to be held on the matter even though there was an injunction prohibiting it. An appeal against the election was drawn up to the federal court in El Reno, but the young lawyer that was supposed to take the paperwork there instead mailed it. The appeal arrived too late and the injunction was lifted. The residents of Cloud Chief were so incensed that they tarred and feathered the young man and ran him out of town.

The county seat was then moved to Cordell after the election, but the fight wasn't yet over. The case was still making its way through the court system, and in 1904 the Supreme Court of the United States maintained that election had been held illegally and ordered the county seat be moved back to Cloud Chief. At that, two County Commissioners from Cordell traveled to Washington and worked a bill through Congress to legalize the election. Finally, President Theodore Roosevelt signed the bill and the fight for the Washita County seat was over.

Cloud Chief was essentially over, too. Without the prospects of the seat returning, business and population dwindled. By 1913, a cotton gin, wagon yard, hotel, and two small stores were all the remained. Today, there are just a few homes still lingering about and a handful of unused decrepit buildings.

There are some other ghost towns around Oklahoma that may be considered a bit more quirky in nature. Retrop was settled around 1896, and was a rolling prairie with cotton and corn fields and a number of small half dugout houses where the farmers and their families lived. It was named as such because a man named Porter had made an application for a post office there to be named after him, but since there was already an office in Indian Territory of the same name, the post office department elected to spell the new one backward. This is also true of the ghost town named Yewed.

The Retrop community built a small 14 x 25 building for a school named Pleasant Hill, which doubled as a church when they could manage to get a preacher. Trouble brewed nearby in a town called Wood, but Wood was soon abandoned after the saloon killing of a Mr. Rush Arter. As more people filtered west, a small town began to grow at Retrop. In the early 1900s, Dr. G. W. Murphy settled there for six years and served the community by making house calls day and night in his old buggy. A consolidated school was formed in 1912, and by 1928 a brick building for it was constructed.

This is the condition of many of the buildings in Retrop.

By the 1940s, Retrop was thriving with a general store, café, barber shop, creamery, laundry, garage, cotton gin, churches, Masonic Lodge, and the Eastern Star Ladies Home Demonstration Club. However, the town was not easily accessible, and as transportation by road became more emphasized this became an increasing problem. Businesses and residents began to move away, the consolidated school closed in 1957, and the Baptist church building near the Retrop Cemetery was uprooted and moved up the road to Sentinel to be used as a residence. While there are still a few people that live in Retrop, the road of the old town site is littered with crumbling buildings. Ironically, when State Routes 6 and 55 were finally established past Retrop they probably would have saved the town, but it was already too late.

Finally, don't blink as you pass through Big Cedar. Seriously. Although it probably never was home to more than fifty people at one time, the hamlet has some historic significance. It once boasted a post office inside a general store, black smith shop, gristmill, saw mill, and cotton gin, all of which, save the store and saw mill, were gone by 1913. For a time in the 1930s, some industry there picked up as white oaks were cut for barrel staves, but this, too, was gone by 1940 and only the general store survived. Yet, none of these bear the significance of Big Cedar.

U.S. Highway 59 was built as an intra-continental highway, spanning from Monterrey, Mexico, to Winnipeg, Canada. Upon its completion in 1961, of all the places to choose along the route, President John F. Kennedy gave a speech celebrating the moment at Big Cedar in front of a throng of 20,000 people. The town had never seen such a thing and a monument was erected to commemorate the event. There's nothing more than the remnants of a service station across from the monument now, but the ghost of President Kennedy's words still echo upon the air:

> "A sympathetic understanding and sound evaluation of present day conditions in Oklahoma necessitates a knowledge of the salient facts of the state's history, for the historical development of any locality determines in large measure the present social conditions of the given region and furnishes a key to an understanding of its peculiar characteristics. The history of Oklahoma has been a unique one, romantic, and in some respects tragic."

Chapter Thirty-Three

Ghost Hunting in Oklahoma

In my last book, *Ghosts of Maryland*, I included a chapter on ghost hunting, which was a rundown of some basic do's and don'ts of investigating and a few tips from those with some experience in the field. Since that time, I have become part of the paranormal team known as Oklahoma Paranormal Research and Investigations (OKPRI) and I'm also a member of the Society of the Haunted. I feel I can now speak to this subject with a more experienced viewpoint. I also want to retain an Oklahoma slant throughout this section, so what I did was ask the group members a number of questions that pertained to paranormal investigating, specifically in the state. Consider this chapter like a panel discussion about what it's like to be a paranormal investigator in Oklahoma.

OKPRI had been a diverse group with many talents. The organization has been in operation for over ten years, and its members have been featured on SyFy's *Ghost Hunters* and Animal Planet's *The Haunted*. Most members at the time of this discussion are now members of the Society of the Haunted, but this is how the team had been constructed:

Christy Clark: Founder and Psychic
Cathy Nance: Case Manager
Chris Borthick: Theologian & Occult Specialist
Mike Ricksecker: Ghostorian
Taylor Nance: Lead Technician
Logan Corelli: Parapsychologist & Case Closer
Dustin Cupit: Researcher & Technician
Johnny Longan: Investigator

OKPRI at the 101 Ranch, October 2010. From left to right: Cathy, Dustin, Christy, Taylor, Logan, and Mike.

All of us investigate, collect evidence, and document our findings, which is standard procedure for anyone that is a part of the team.

We all got started in this field for a variety of reasons, and none of them include getting a quick thrill or hoping to get on television. Many of us had unusual experiences as children. Cathy lived in an environment in which paranormal activity surrounded her, but she accepted it as normal since she was a very spiritual person. She believes the trigger for much of this activity was a number of near death experiences at the age of three. As she grew older and began to understand that most other people were not like her, she became extremely curious and started to explore the possibilities. Her son, Taylor, has also seen things he couldn't explain since about the age of eight.

Christy was born with spiritual gifts, likely through her Native American heritage, that were largely excused away by her mother and pastor in her very Christian home. They repeatedly told her that her mind was playing tricks on her and ghosts weren't real. She recounted,

"Afraid of their talks of a burning hell, I tried to ignore and forget about my gifts, however, as I grew older I still retained my interest and curiosity about the paranormal and decided to take up the study and learn more about the abilities I possess." After her initial investigations in local cemeteries revealed some fantastic audio and photographic evidence, she formed OKPRI in June 2000.

Chris Borthick has had an interest in alternative religions and spiritual views ever since he graduated from college. He was part of a metaphysical discussion group when he attended his first ghost hunt at the Blue Belle Saloon in Guthrie and had a number of interesting personal experiences there, as well as capturing his first piece of photographic evidence. He explained how his interest in paranormal investigation increased, "Ghost hunting seemed to be a natural extension of my interest in that side of life, and through paranormal investigation I have grown spiritually and expanded my knowledge of metaphysics."

My initial interest is a combination of a number of things. First of all, I have always had an interest in God and the spiritual world from a young age. During my First Communion as a Roman Catholic, I was so focused on the ceremony that I didn't even realize that as I sat next to the divider of the elongated pew in which I settled that my family and best friend had found a seat right there beside me on the other side of the divider. Shortly thereafter, I became an altar boy and participated in readings at the alternate second services at the church. Twenty years later I was performing communion meditations at a Christian church in Frederick, Maryland.

Over all these years, however, other things happened. As a child, I experienced something in the middle of the night that was largely explained away as a dream, although I know I was wide awake. A number of the dreams that I did have were themed about the afterlife. My creativity bent this way as well as I wrote small mystery stories and then, at the age of eleven, relished in creating a "haunting" at my grandparents' house to first scare the neighbor kid and then my sister and cousin (soon all four of us had a fantastic romp with it for years that is still a family legend to this day). Curiosity about ghosts really kicked up when my mother bought me *Yankee Ghosts* by Hans Holzer, and, finally, in high school when I read *The Amityville Horror*. Instead of being frightened of what I read, I shocked the wits out of my girlfriend when I stated, "I want to go to that house and see what's really there." A young paranormal investigator was budding.

As a collective unit, the team sets out on dozens of investigations across Oklahoma, and even into other states, each year. Some have been absolutely fantastic while others were quite dubious, which is the nature of the territory, but everyone has their favorite Oklahoma haunt. For quite a few in the group that location is Guthrie and The Stone Lion Inn. Cathy loves the history, old buildings, and ambiance of Guthrie itself, while I love the mysterious feel and ongoing activity at The Stone Lion Inn. "The Stone Lion Inn is my favorite location at the moment in Oklahoma," Chris elaborated. "I have had personal experiences that I believe were the little girl in the attic brushing my hand and the cold sensation of her staying next to me while in the attic. I also have seen shadow movement there in the main hall, and with some of my fellow investigators had a literal creaky door in the haunted house experience."

Christy, Chris, and Dustin are ready to give a presentation at the Stone Lion Inn.

Cathy also places the house in Eldorado featured on *The Haunted* at the top of her list and considers the home the most negative place she's been. Taylor's favorite haunt is the Masonic temple in Muskogee, "because that has been the first time I saw an apparition and the first time I also got immediate responses to questions."

Christy gives her nod to an old Indian boarding school west of Oklahoma City. "In the children's dorms we actually heard voices of children calling out to us telling us to follow them and to come find them. We also experienced seeing strange shadows and white apparitions roaming the hallways and rooms of several of the old buildings."

While those may be favorites, other things make a location more memorable. Cathy and Christy both cite Eldorado as their most unforgettable location. According to Cathy, "Eldorado had a palpable energy to the place. You felt watched and knew that what was there did not want you there. I was going up the stairs by myself and felt something on the back of my neck breathing. That feeling made me slam my back against the wall and I had to laugh to shake the emotions I was feeling." She also opened a secret hidden area under the stairs that was furnished and had wall paper in a style that was decades old.

Christy elaborates, "When the homeowners first contacted us about coming out to do this investigation, they had already previously experienced several strange things such as swarms of flies appearing in their kitchen then suddenly disappearing, bad odors, disembodies voices, apparitions, things moving, footsteps, dogs dying and/or becoming very ill, and much more. The family believed they had a demon in their home however my group and I went to the location with an open mind and no preconceived judgments of what we would find. Needless to say, this investigation turned out to be the scariest for me due to myself coming under spiritual attack and then one of my investigators who tried to help me was physically attacked and rendered unconscious for a little over four minutes. Phenomenal evidence was recorded from this location and a good friend of mine and well known demonologist, Carl Johnson, was brought in to help us assist the family in getting rid of the negative entity we believed to be a possible demonic spirit."

The house in Eldorado isn't the only spine-chilling location the team has investigated. Taylor recalls a restaurant in Muskogee where he was physically touched. "Chris and I were the only ones in the restaurant and we were sitting at the bar when all of a sudden I felt a sharp pain in my lower back. When I told Chris I was in pain the wine glasses hanging at the bar started clinking together, and then I heard footsteps going back into the bar." It was revealed moments later that the sharp pain was a set of scratch marks that somehow appeared on Taylor's back.

Taylor was also the subject of Chris's most memorable investigation at a location that became nicknamed "The House of the Insane." On this particular night we were interacting with the spirit of a young boy when Taylor asked if the boy would play with him. Chris continues the story, "About thirty minutes later Taylor discovered his keys were missing and the entire team tore through the house looking for them to no avail. We went out into the yard, by the cars, and came back in the house and checked some of the equipment bags. I watched Taylor look inside a pelican equipment bag before we headed into another bedroom to search.

Electronic devices are helpful in investigating the paranormal.

"I addressed the house and said, 'That's enough, you've had your fun.'" Taylor echoed that next to me.

"We heard Cathy cry out from the front room, 'Are these them?'"

"We moved into the room and sure enough, there were his keys.

"'Where were they?'

"Cathy responded, 'In the pelican bag.'

"That event, coupled with a skin-tingling high EMF in the room where the little boy's ghost was and later that same night the sensation I had of being touched that produced a K-II spike, makes (House of the Insane) a memorable location."

Ghost hunting in Oklahoma is challenging because of the great distances one must travel to a number of the locations. Outside of the cities of Oklahoma City and Tulsa, the population starts getting rather sparse. There are some fantastic small towns rich in history and the paranormal, but they take quite a deal of planning to drive to. We've had some interesting trips bounding across the countryside, not quite sure if we were headed in the right direction, but the team has lived to tell the tales. We also quite enjoy a variety of foods along the way.

One of our most legendary crazy road trips was a trip down to Caddo, which Chris likes to call "Lost in Southeast Oklahoma." We were taking the "scenic" route down to the town and got a bit misdirected along the way. Cathy was on the phone with the homeowner and he was telling us that we needed to do things like, "turn left at the divot in the road," and made comments in his country twang such as, "man, you're way up there," and, "I don't know where you are." We were also baffled at the wild life we saw, which included giant birds lingering in the middle of the road, a giant black dog that lunged at the car and missed, and some creature in a small pond that may have been a llama or alpaca, but looked eerily reminiscent of the Loch Ness Monster. Between divots, birds, and Nessie, we had laughs all the way to Caddo.

Somewhere along the legendary road trip to Caddo.

Cathy's favorite road trip was actually one out of state to the Villisca axe murder house in Iowa, but her favorite Oklahoma trip was to Muskogee. "That town has some craziness to it, especially at the fast food drive up windows. I will never forget Lenny! Let me say that there are several restaurants we liked to eat at that sadly have closed. The food was amazing!"

With over a decade of experience, Christy has been on countless numbers of road trips and says that while she doesn't have a specific favorite road trip, she has enjoyed them all. "I will say that some of the funniest times we have are spent talking about particular road trips with a former member who drove like a child riding a roller coaster. Our team had some great laughs recalling the times our members rolled onto the floorboard of his vehicle, slammed into the seat in front of them, or hit the nearest window they were sitting next to."

She also enjoys it when we spend travel time reviewing recorded evidence, preparing for another investigation, or just conversing, telling jokes, and laughing.

OKPRI and the Society of the Haunted are mostly scientific organizations, bringing along a number of meters and devices to detect anomalous activity that could be paranormal. One of the biggest thrills of investigating spirit activity is capturing something on an audio or visual medium that we can say is truly evidence. Devices the team uses include various EMF detectors, temperature gauges, audio recorders, digital cameras, video cameras, and a complete DVR system with night vision. Without capturing evidence on these devices it is almost impossible to try and prove our findings to the homeowners and skeptics.

The favorite device within the group is the audio recorder. We have all captured a number of electronic voice phenomena (EVPs) that cannot be explained by anyone else speaking or radio waves, and it is especially gratifying when an EVP backs up a personal experience such as hearing a disembodied voice whisper a specific word. A number of us enjoy taking photographs as well, although it takes scores upon scores of photographs to be shot before that one piece of solid photographic evidence is captured. Cathy and I also enjoy capturing video, but others will pick up a handheld video camera as well and start recording. Chris and I have also liked using the K-II meter and Chris will also bring along an assortment of crystals that may give off an various vibrations if spirits are near.

Each investigator has successfully captured a vast amount of paranormal evidence with these devices. One of the first pieces Christy ever captured was what looks like a portal at a cemetery near Earlsboro. It resembles a large veil-splitting anomaly with a solid vertical white line and several light streaks shooting out of it. She considers one of her best EVPs to be that of a little girl reacting to the homeowners bringing in pizza at a residence in Tulsa by loudly whining, "Aw, I want my din-din." There were no children in the home.

OKPRI members are hard at work examining evidence, organizing cases, and adding information to the website.

The team has captured a variety of shadows and light anomalies with both digital cameras and video recorders. In an interesting combination of device evidence, Chris, Taylor, and Johnny were utilizing a K-II meter in a house in south Oklahoma City while I had left an audio recorder in the room. They were asking a spirit to light up the K-II and each time it lit up, my audio recorder about six feet away recorded a buzzing sound. The most interesting of these interactions was when they were asking the entity to keep the K-II lights red, which it did over the course of a minute, and the entire time my audio recorder picked up the buzzing sound. The audio recorder also picked up a number of EVPs during that time in response to the questions they were asking.

There are a number of different ways to run a paranormal group, and with so many teams now popping up all across the nation, the variety of styles can be observed everywhere. One of the great debates amongst these groups is the difference in using mediums and psychics and keeping the investigation purely scientific.

Here's how we used Christy, our psychic. When OKPRI began an investigation, Christy remained out of the loop. She was not given any background information of the location, and when the group arrived at a location she at first remained outside and stayed quite far away (much to her chagrin on cold winter days). After interviewing the homeowner or caretaker of the property and getting a tour of the active areas, Christy was then brought in to perform her own walk-through. This was usually just a small team that included the case manager and someone to jot down Christy's impressions in a notebook. On a high percentage of occasions, her impressions of the activity were quite dead on with most of what the team members were told in the interview.

These psychic impressions are not only helpful with confirming the location's stories, but there is additional information she's able to pick up on that helps us in research. Perhaps a name is given or an event that transpired long ago that we're able to follow up and find through our investigation of the location's history and the previous owners. A better picture of the haunting and why it's occurring is then discovered.

Thorough research can uncover any number of things, or even debunk some claims, and is why I'm an avid advocate of it. A residual haunting of a crying woman could possibly be explained by the fact that a previous homeowner had an infant pass away, a birth she never talked about to local friends and neighbors. The rumor of a boy dying on the stairs gets debunked when there's no record of a boy that age ever living there, nor any sort of accident report. Or, perhaps, some negative energy is brought into the home because it's discovered that a previous homeowner accidentally killed a pedestrian crossing the road while he or she was driving. The possibilities are endless.

What is for certain is that Oklahoma is loaded with painful history that makes it an extremely paranormal state. Native American spirits that the group encounters can date back hundreds of years, as Cathy describes, "For over six hundred years Oklahoma was the cultural center of the United States. It then became a virtual waste land and outlaw territory. It was the place of wars between Native American tribes. The Trail of Tears led to Oklahoma with the forcible relocation of Indians from their ancestral homes. Many died along the way and those that didn't were angry."

Chris once encountered a Native American tribe on one person's land and observed shadow shapeshifters on reservation acreage. With many Indian villages and burial grounds lost to time and scattered throughout the state, an encounter with a Native American spirit is not uncommon.

There are plenty of other spirits that are connected to people, homes, businesses, and land throughout Oklahoma as well. With the state's diverse background, one may encounter the ghost of a ranch hand just as likely as Anna Overholser. Chris points out, "Locations are well documented with ghosts of settlers, pioneers, brothel employees, and other characters. Additionally immigrants from different nationalities with different religions and beliefs have brought their beliefs and spirits with them."

With a plethora of activity from a variety of sources around the state of Oklahoma, the team has had quite a few interesting personal experiences. Chris and Taylor point to Taylor's incident of being scratched and the rattling of the glasses behind the bar in Muskogee as their most memorable personal experience. Cathy's was working with Carl Johnson on the Eldorado case and assisting him with the cleansing. She'll never forget spraying holy water around the backyard and watching shadow people running from the house and scampering up the trees. What I experienced at The Stone Lion Inn in May 2010 still holds as my favorite personal experience. There was just so much going on that night with the drawer closing on its own, the picture falling off the wall, the door moving on the second floor, and the rush of energy that hit me in the library.

Getting device activity deep in the bowels of the 101 Ranch's white house.

Christy's most memorable personal experience is rather different than the rest of ours. It's a lengthy account, so I'll let her tell it in her own words:

"I have to say my most favorite personal experience took place at a residential investigation in Nicoma Park, Oklahoma. This experience was more of a psychic experience and connection I had rather than a physical interaction experience. I came in connection with the spirit of a 27-year-old man named Mark who shared his story and emotions with me. He was murdered by a young woman who was madly in love with him and who wanted them to be together, but his feelings weren't reciprocated back towards her, so in a fit of jealously and anger she murdered him.

"Mark showed me a time back in August 1977 when he was getting ready to lie down and take a nap. His wife and toddler son were out running errands that day and were not present in the home during the time of his murder. As he was getting on the bed, this young woman, named Alicia, came up behind him and stabbed him three times in the back. Mark fell onto the bed, his arm hanging off with blood seeping from his body. A couple of hours later his family came home and his young son came in the room to wake him up. Horrified, Mark stood outside his body in spirit watching as his young son called out to him and began to cry when Mark's lifeless body didn't respond. Mark's spirit stood there with his arms reaching out to his son assuring him he was still there with him. It was at that point that Mark dumped all of his emotional turmoil on me and I began bawling uncontrollably.

"I did research and found where Mark was buried and that there had been an identical murder at the home back in August 1977 of a young man that matched the description of Mark. Mark's last request was that he be connected again with his son, but my research led me to a dead end, and I could never find his boy. It has been several years since I connected with Mark, but I will never forget that investigation, nor the things he showed me and allowed me to feel. It was quite memorable and a memory that will forever stick with me."

Every day there are numerous calls placed to Oklahoma Paranormal Research and Investigations and the Society of the Haunted by people looking for answers and help with whatever strange activity may be going on in their homes. Many times these things can be explained away by some physical, tangible, and logical reason. However, for all those other times that it can't be explained away, that all the attempts to provide a reasonable explanation prove fruitless, our team is right there to help.

Final Thoughts

After my original submission of this manuscript, what had been Oklahoma Paranormal Research and Investigations during my research and writing came to an abrupt end. Due to a number of unresolvable differences of opinion in the direction of the group Cathy, Chris, Dustin, Johnny, Logan, Taylor, Andrew (a part-time videographer not yet mentioned), and I left to form the Society of the Haunted. The details of that event are irrelevant to the scope of this book, but parts of the manuscript suddenly became awkward to retain, especially Chapter 33.

However, I believe that it would have been a disservice to the reader to remove certain portions of the book based upon the inability of a group of people to find common ground. Thus, the content of the book has remained intact with a few strategic changes in phraseology. With that said, we can now return to our regularly scheduled final thoughts.

One of the things I'm most commonly asked is, "Have you heard of <insert name of ghost and location here>?"

Given the wide breadth of locales that claim to have paranormal activity, especially in a state the size of Oklahoma, there's a chance I haven't. That's the wonderful thing about this field. There's always another story somewhere. Feel free to tell it.

Writing about ghosts, legends, hauntings, and anything paranormal is an ongoing project. As long as someone is willing to dig for them more tales and secrets are waiting to be uncovered. Additional material to draw from also becomes available with each passing day as history is constantly being made. Such is the way of time.

What does the future hold for paranormal investigators? That's a good question. Paranormal teams are sprouting up all over the country and more people are now willing to come forth with their experiences in their home, place of work, or location they've visited. Due to this, the field will continue to develop exponentially in the coming years.

This newfound openness will create a influx of new ghost stories. Many of these will be true while many will be debunked. What's key to keep in mind is that these stories all originated somewhere, whether that be from an old tale that Aunt Polly liked to recite, a long-lost document newly found, or the recent death of a loved one.

And as a ghostorian, original truth is what I will continue to seek.

Haunted Atlas of Oklahoma

This guide is divided into four quarter sections of Oklahoma and also includes city maps of Guthrie and Oklahoma City. The ghost stories and hauntings from each section of the book have their respective locations marked on the corresponding map as well as cemeteries and ghost towns I've mentioned throughout the text. I've tossed in a couple of other notable ones that you may also pique your interest.

Should you use the information here to plan out your next ghost hunting excursion, please keep in mind that some of these locations are private property and permission to visit will be needed. There are sixty locations listed!

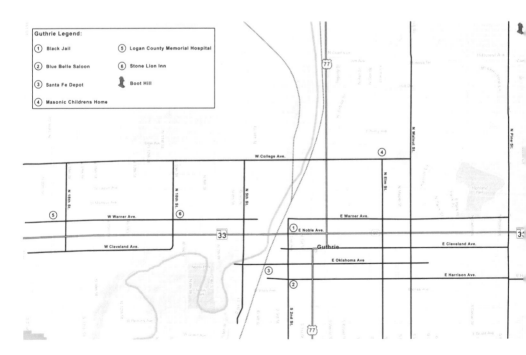

Guthrie Legend:

1. Black Jail
2. Blue Belle Saloon
3. Santa Fe Depot
4. Masonic Childrens Home
5. Logan County Memorial Hospital
6. Stone Lion Inn
- Boot Hill

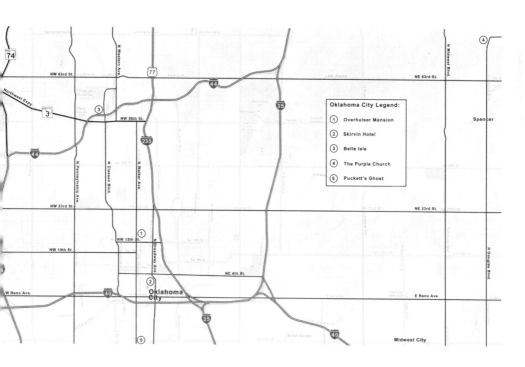

Oklahoma City Legend:

1. Overholser Mansion
2. Skirvin Hotel
3. Belle Isle
4. The Purple Church
5. Puckett's Ghost

Northeast Oklahoma

Cemeteries

1. Cowboy Hill
2. Dick Duck Cemetery
3. Fort Gibson

Ghost Towns

1. Ingalls
2. Picher
3. Shamrock
4. Tahlonteeskee

Haunted Locations

1. 101 Ranch
2. Constantine Theater
3. Brady Theater
4. Gilcrease Museum and Home
5. Belvidere Mansion
6. Labadie Mansion

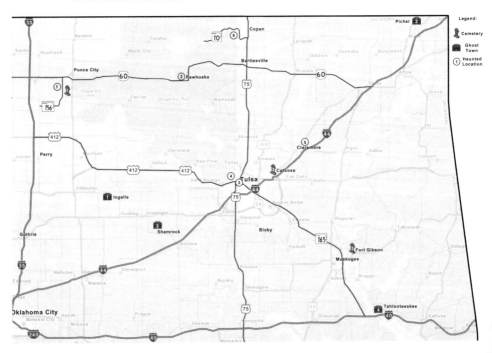

Southeast Oklahoma

Cemeteries

1. Earlsboro Cemetery
2. Fort Washita
3. Kowana Cemetery
4. Romulus Cemetery

Ghost Towns

1. Big Cedar
2. Earlsboro
3. Maud

Haunted Locations

1. Fort Washita
2. Ritz Theater
3. Eskridge Hotel
4. Sense of Charm

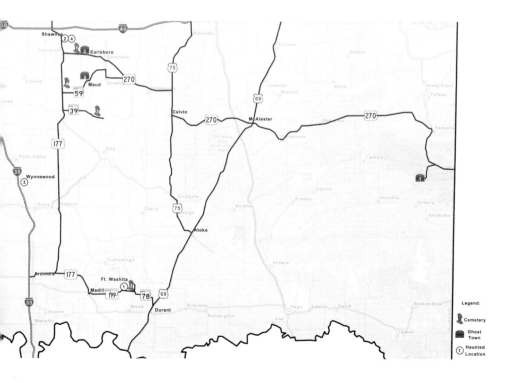

Northwest Oklahoma

Cemeteries

1. Arapaho Cemetery
2. Black Bear Cemetery
3. Elmwood Cemetery
4. Frisco Cemetery
5. Imo Cemetery

Ghost Towns

1. Frisco
2. Ingersoll
3. Reno City
4. Yewed

Haunted Locations

1. Garfield Furniture
2. Knox Building
3. Black Bear Church and Cemetery
4. Route 66, El Reno
5. Woodward Hospital

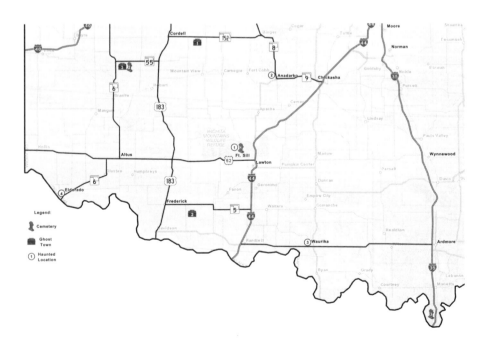

Southwest Oklahoma

Cemeteries

1. Apache Prisoner of War Cemetery
2. Retrop Cemetery
3. Thackerville Cemetery

Ghost Towns

1. Cloud Chief
2. Loveland
3. Retrop

Haunted Locations

1. Fort Sill
2. Riverside Indian School
3. Nancy's Antiques
4. "Leave or Die" House

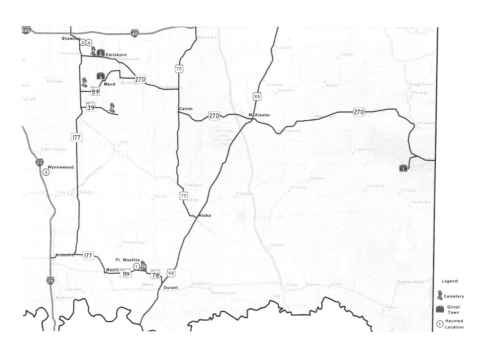

Glossary

Anomaly: An irregularity; a deviation from the normal or usual order, type, etc.

Apparition: A spectral image, projection, or manifestation of an entity.

Cleansing: The purification of a dwelling from malevolent entities.

Digital video recorder (DVR): A device that records video and stores it onto a hard disk in digital format.

Electromagnetic field (EMF): A region in space through which energy passes that has been created by electrically charged particles. EMFs are produced by such things as power lines, electric appliances, radio waves, and microwaves.

Electronic Voice Phenomena (EVP): Disembodied voices captured by audio recording devices.

Entity: A disembodied consciousness that may also be referred to as a ghost or a spirit.

Gauss: Named after Karl Friedrich Gauss, it is the unit of magnetic flux density in the centimeter-gram-second system equal to one maxwell per square centimeter, or 10^{-4} tesla.

Gaussmeter: A magnetometer whose scale is graduated in gauss or kilogauss, and usually measures only the intensity, and not the direction, of the magnetic field.

Ghost: A generic term used for the entity of a paranormal occurrence.

Haunting: Repeated paranormal phenomena in a specific location.

Intelligent haunt: A type of haunting in which the entity is aware of its surroundings and interacts freely with humans and the environment.

K-II meter: A type of meter that measures electromagnetic fields (EMF) using a series of lights.

Metaphysics: The philosophical study of the nature of reality.

Orb: In the paranormal field, a true orb is a sphere of energy, usually translucent white but many have bluish or reddish hues.

Paranormal: Something that is beyond normal explanation.

Parapsychology: The study of mental phenomena beyond the scope of normal physical explanation.

Poltergeist: German for "noisy ghost," it is a haunting in which random objects are moved about in order to draw attention to the entity.

Portal: Believed to be an inter-dimensional doorway which allows entities access to our world.

Psychic: Relating to the psyche of the mind or soul, refers to a person who sensitive beyond normal means.

Residual haunt: A type of haunting in which the original entity is no longer present, but it's energy has been left behind and it periodically plays back events like a recording device.

Spirit: A consciousness or existence apart from the physical world, the life-force of an organism, also refers to a ghost or entity.

Tri-Field Meter: An electromagnetic field (EMF) meter with both magnetic and electric settings

Vortex: An anomaly that appears as a translucent white tube or funnel in photographs.

Bibliography

Aiken, Charlotte. "Moore Man Falls To Death Inside Abandoned Power Plant." *The Daily Oklahoman*, October 31, 1999.

Associated Press. "70 Negroes, 10 Whites die In Rioting." *The Daily Oklahoman*, June 2, 1921.

"Bandit Slain in Desperate Fight With Officers." *The Daily Oklahoman*, October 8, 1911.

Bates, Finis L. *The Escape and Suicide of John Wilkes Booth.* Parkersburg, West Virginia: The White Publishing Co., 1908.

Bittner, J. B. Blosser. "Woman Seeks Cousin Lost After Tornado." *The Daily Oklahoman*, April 13, 1998.

"Booth Story Is Alive Again." *The Daily Oklahoman*, January 16, 1904.

Bouziden, Deborah. *Off The Beaten Path: Oklahoma.* Guilford, Connecticut: The Globe Pequot Press, 2007.

Breece, Melissa. "Urban Legends." OKWU Eagle, http://www.okwueagle.com/playground/2007/03/30/urban-legends

Churchill, April and Kizer-Dennis, Dorothy. *Claremore.* Chicago, Illinois: Arcadia Publishing, 2007.

"Coffelt Trial." *The Daily Oklahoman*, June 12, 1902.

Collings, Ellsworth and England, Alma Miller. *The 101 Ranch.* Norman, Oklahoma: University of Oklahoma Press, 1937.

"Cotton Gin Cases Soon To Be Tried." *The Daily Oklahoman*, June 13, 1913.

Curly. "William M. 'Bill' Doolin." http://www.badhombres.com/outlaws/bill-doolin.htm

"Death Strikes Twice At One State Family." *The Daily Oklahoman*, September 5, 1949.

Dennis, Frank L. "Two Die In Guthrie Train Wreck." *The Daily Oklahoman*, May 31, 1936.

"Deputy Hold Officer While Throat is Cut." *The Daily Oklahoman*, April 14, 1908.

Drowatzky, Sheridan B. "Waurika." Oklahoma Historical Society's Encyclopedia of History & Culture, http://digital.library.okstate.edu/encyclopedia/entries/W/WA048.html

Erwin, Sarah. "Gilcrease Museum." Oklahoma Historical Society's Encyclopedia of History & Culture, http://digital.library.okstate.edu/encyclopedia/entries/G/GI004.html

"Father's Right To Kill Is Upheld." *The Daily Oklahoman*, September 22, 1912.

"Feud Claims Third Victim." *The Daily Oklahoman*, April 12, 1910.

Goodwin, David. "Fort Washita." Military Ghosts, http://www.militaryghosts.com/washita.html.

Grimm, Steve. "Bluford 'Blue' Duck." Wild West History Association, http://wildwesthistory.org/research/bios/Duck_Bluford.asp

"G. W. Miller Denies." *The Daily Oklahoman*, February 1, 1902.

Hacker, Tonya and Wilson, Tammy. *Ghostlahoma.* Decatur, Illinois: Whitechapel Press, 2009.

HauntedHouses.com. "Mason's Children's Home." http://www.hauntedhouses.com/states/ok/mason_childrens_home.cfm

Hiatt, Robert R. "The Ghost of Fort Sill." Invisible Ink. http://www.invink.com/x253.html

"Hotel Officer Saves Woman From Long Drop." *The Daily Oklahoman*, August 2, 1939.

Jensen, Richard D. *The Amazing Tom Mix: The Most Famous Cowboy of the Movies.* Lincoln, Nebraska: iUniverse, 2005.

Lackmeyer, Steve. "Girl, 12, Injured In Fall At Belle Isle Power Plant." *The Daily Oklahoman*, January 8, 1995.

"Legacy That Refused to End." *The Oklahoman*. January 28, 2007.

Lackmeyer, Steve and Money, Jack. *Skirvin.* Full Circle, 2009.

Lamb, Arthur H. *Tragedies of the Osage Hills*. Pawhuska, Oklahoma: The Osage Printery.

Langston, Carol. "Outlaw's Strange Odyssey Ending At Last." *The Daily Oklahoman*, April 14, 1977.

Lassila, Kathrin Day and Branch, Mark Alden. "Whose Skull and Bones?" Yale Alumni Magazine, http://www.yalealumnimagazine.com/issues/2006_05/notebook.html

Logan Medical Center. "History of Medical Institutes in Guthrie." http://www.loganmedicalcenter.com/lmc.nsf/View/History

"Man Dies In Hotel Plunge." *The Daily Oklahoman*, October 14, 1932.

"Man Vanishes in City Lake After Picnic." *The Daily Oklahoma*, June 11, 1938.

May, Jon D. "Fort Washita." Oklahoma Historical Society's Encyclopedia of History & Culture, http://digital.library.okstate.edu/encyclopedia/entries/f/fo046.html.

Medley, Robert. "Guthrie Homes Ghostly." *The Daily Oklahoman*, October 30, 1989.

Morris, John W. *Ghost Towns of Oklahoma*. Norman, Oklahoma: University of Oklahoma Press, 1978.

Nash, Bridget. "Stories of Paranormal, Hauntings Abound in Enid." *The Enid News and Eagle*, http://enidnews.com/localnews/x518699447/Stories-of-paranormal-hauntings-abound-in-Enid?keyword=topstory

National Historic Route 66 Federation. "History of Route 66." http://www.national66.com/66hstry.html.

Norman, Michael and Scott, Beth. *Historic Haunted America*. New York, New York: Tor, 1995.

Oklahoma Paranormal Research and Investigations. "Blue Belle Saloon." http://www.okpri.com/BlueBelleSaloon.htm

Oklahoma Paranormal Research and Investigations. "The Historical Eskridge Hotel." http://www.okpri.com/EskridgeHotel.html

Oklahoma Paranormal Research and Investigations. "The Historical Ritz Theater." http://www.okpri.com/RitzTheater.html

Oklahoma Paranormal Research and Investigations. "The House in Eldorado." http://www.okpri.com/EldoradoHouse.html

Oklahoma Paranormal Research and Investigations. "Sense of Charm." http://www.okpri.com/SenseofCharms.html

"Officers Probing Scherubel Death." *The Daily Oklahoman*, April 19, 1913.

Parr, Ray. "3,000 Are Left Homeless; Loss Is $5 Millions In Storm." *The Daily Oklahoman*, April 11, 1947.

"Passing of Cowboy Cause of Grief To A Plainsman Who Preceeded Tenderfoot." *The Daily Oklahoman*, April 19, 1908.

Price, Christian. "Man's Death Prompts Town Legend." News 9, http://www.news9.com/global/story.asp?s=8732815&ClientType=Printable

Rock Island & Pacific Railroad. "History." http://www.rockrail.com/history.html

Rogers County Historical Society. "The Belvidere Mansion Another Claremore Treasure." http://www.rogerscountyhistory.org/belvidere_mansion/bm.html.

Sarchet, Corb. "Chaos in the Coffee Cups." *The Daily Oklahoman*, July 19, 1953.

"Spirits Summoned To Material World." *The Daily Oklahoman*, March 16, 1919.

Sutter, Ellie. "Guthrie Link To Koresh Seen As Possibility." *The Daily Oklahoman*, October 16, 1993.

Taylor, Troy. *Ghost Hunter's Guidebook*. Decatur, Illinois: Whitechapel Press, 2007.

Thetford, Francis. "Old Railroader Scorned Toughs." *The Daily Oklahoman*, September 25, 1968.

"Tornado Mystery Grows! Who Took Child, 4, From Hospital?" *The Daily Oklahoman*, June 5, 1947.

Wallis, Michael. *Pretty Boy: The Life and Times of Charles Arthur Floyd*. New York, New York: St. Martin's Press, 1992.

Warlick, Heather. "Ghost Tales Pique Interest In Historic Inn." *The Oklahoman*, October 30, 2006.

Weiser, Kathy. "Gilcrease Museum – History & Haunting." *Legends of America*, http://www.legendsofamerica.com/ok-gilcreasemuseum.html.

"Oklahoma Legends: Ghostly Tales of Oklahoma 66." *Legends of America*, http://www.legendsofamerica.com/66-okghosts.html

"Wild West Show." *The Daily Oklahoman*, April 11, 1905.

Wilson, Connie. "A True Ghost Story From 'Ghostly Tales of Route 66' and the Fort El Reno Ghost T Associated Content, http://www.associatedcontent.com/article/2254067/a_true_ghost_story ghostly_tales.html

Wilson, Linda D. "Fraternal Orders." Oklahoma Historical Society's Encyclopedia of History f http://digital.library.okstate.edu/encyclopedia/entries/F/FR007.html

"Woman Falls To Death At Park." *The Daily Oklahoman*, August 2, 1926.

Index